Rowdy Rising

Published by Fifth Estate Media, Maitland, Florida

www.nonfictionpublish.com

FIFTH ESTATE media

Printed in the United States of America

Cover photograph, 1985 Pulitzer Prize collection,
by Orange County Register with permissions granted by Zuma Press Inc.
Cover illustration by Jesse Kunerth
Interior photographs provided by Rowdy and Judy Gaines
Foreward by Bob Costas

U.S. Library of Congress cataloging publication

Rowdy Rising
From Rejected to Unrivaled

FOREWORD

Ambrose Gaines, IV.

There. With that out of the way, let's talk about Rowdy Gaines. Here's the big picture: in a variety of ways Rowdy has been a major figure in his sport for nearly forty years. In the late '70s, he was a teenage sensation, eventual five-time NCAA Champion and World Record holder. Headed, it seemed, for the medal podium at the 1980 Moscow Olympics.

When the U.S. boycott of those Games deferred that dream, Rowdy was side-tracked – athletically and emotionally. An afterthought as the 1984 Los Angeles Games approached. A long-shot to even qualify. Instead, Rowdy Gaines won three gold medals and became one of the bold-faced names of an epic American Olympics. A high point, but far from an end point.

Rowdy would later compete in and win Masters swimming championships, setting more records in the process. He would coach and mentor young swimmers, act as a tireless ambassador for the sport and remain a highly visible and influential part of the Olympics as NBC's primary swimming analyst for the last seven Summer Games, beginning with Barcelona in 1992.

Cue up the tape of any big Olympic swimming moment of the last two decades, including all of Michael Phelps' history-making performances, and Rowdy's voice and insight is part of it. His knowledge, not only of the competition itself, but of the competitors themselves, is encyclopedic. He is clearly astute, but more than that – his excitement is genuine…and infectious.

Among his colleagues, Rowdy is universally respected. Always prepared. Simultaneously passionate and professional. And, old school as it may sound, he is a gentleman. Unfailingly courteous, generous with his time and eager to be part of a successful team.

For a long time now, millions have appreciated Rowdy as an athlete and a broadcaster. What relatively few have known is how interesting his life's story is. Turns out there has been more than a bit of choppy water along the way.

So *Rowdy Rising* takes readers beyond the dark-horse podium glory of 1984 and goes on to examine Gaines' lifelong immersion in what, when you think about it, may be the world's oldest sport. Everything from childhood swims in gator-infested neighborhood lakes to his struggles with sudden paralysis and then recovery from life-threatening Guillain-Barres Syndrome, Rowdy's story will engage just about everyone who has ever waded into the water.

On these pages, Rowdy also emphasizes the critical need for infant and youth swim lessons. It's a breezy read that may serve as an inspiration for some kid, somewhere, who flounders in high school or for the countless adults who still look to the water for the challenges and rewards it can bring.

The birth certificate may say Ambrose Gaines, IV. But in many ways Rowdy Gaines is one of a kind. Read on and see for yourself.

– Bob Costas

PREFACE

I am not a competitive swimmer. My most accomplished stroke is the doggy paddle. How is it that I should write a book about one of the world's legendary swimmers?

In working alongside Rowdy at The Limu Company, he began to occasionally share parts of his story. It happened fairly regularly, but in pieces. As often as it happened, I ended up continually entertained and interested.

I sensed he was only sharing a small part of who he was. At speaking engagements, he would talk about how he had won some Olympic gold medals and how he'd done so because he refused to give up. All of that was true, of course, but there was so much more to say.

One of the lessons I have picked up as a writer is you should actually have something worth writing about. There has to be a solid, meaty reason for tackling a subject. There has to be a story worth telling. Nobody wants to read a book by someone who "talks loud and says nothing."

Rowdy had a story—a pretty spectacular one—but there were so many unexplored layers of it. It was these layers that helped create the man who became an unparalleled international champion in 1984.

I finally approached him one day. I hit him square between the eyes with an idea. I said, "If you ever get to the point you want to tell your story in its entirety, I'd like to help." I had no real business doing such a thing, but it's something I wanted to tackle all the same. In typical understated Rowdy fashion, he didn't take much time to think about it. He simply said, "Okay, let's do it!" and we were off to those proverbial races.

So many weekends and late weeknights and interviews and road trips and lunches and dinners later, I can say I feel like we've accomplished a good thing. I believe the stories within these pages serve to more fully define a legend and a voice that comes into our homes every fourth summer during the Olympics.

Writing this book hasn't been an easy road, but I suppose no book ever is. One form was nearly released just before the 2012 Olympics, but it was shelved. I sometimes questioned whether or not it would ever get published. Luckily, we've made it past all of that.

I am proud and honored to present you with Rowdy Rising. I hope you come away from it having learned more about a man who chose never to give up on his dreams. I hope it, in turn, encourages you to never give up on yours.

— Dainon Moody

DEDICATION

For Richard Ehlert, my stepdad and friend, who has always urged me to write books.

– Dainon Moody

INTRODUCTION

I undertook this book so that future generations of the Gaines family and others might know my story in a way they otherwise never could. My wife, Judy, is incredible at researching our family's genealogy and it fascinates me to find out about my ancestors. I always thought that Gainesville, Florida was named after a relative of mine but Judy discovered that my eighth great uncle General Edmond Pendleton Gaines founded the town. It floors me to learn that I had an ancestor that was elected to the state senate of Tennessee while in jail! I am a curious person and wanted to know more so I endeavored to learn and leave a written history for future Gaines' generations.

With the advent of the Internet my descendants will find out a lot more about me than I could ever find out about my ancestors, but they won't be able to understand my feelings and emotions.

People come into our lives — some for short periods of time and others for decades. They help shape our values, futures, and contributions to society. My journey, while blessed with the fortune of Olympic glory, is in many ways no different from others. I've had struggles, heartache, frustration, and moments of self-doubt. I made a lot of mistakes. I lost more races than I won. But what has sustained and allowed me to achieve my dreams have been my family, faith and extended family of supporters.

My wife, Judy, and my daughters Emily, Madison, Savanna, and Isabelle have meant more to me than I could ever begin to describe in just a few sentences. I quite frankly would not know where I would be without them. Judy and I have been together for almost three decades. It was love at first sight when I met her in Las Vegas, Nevada. She has been the Rock of Gibraltar with our family. I have chosen the path of being a husband and father who traveled extensively for his job and although I have few regrets in my life, being away so much is certainly one of them. Judy has been that consistent positive influence and for that I am eternally grateful. She still makes me laugh and is the most beautiful woman on the planet. I know retirement for me is around the corner and it will be wonderful to spend the NEXT thirty years just hanging out with her and getting to know her in a whole new way. Isabelle is sixteen and the last one still at home. Once she is off to college it will be party time for Rowdy and Judy! I'm kidding of course, but it will certainly be a new chapter in our lives. Judy is my best friend. She is the love of my life and I am so proud of her. I hope she knows just how much she means to me.

Being a parent is the most difficult job in the world. Being a dad to all girls is, well, there must be a special place in heaven for me! I have at many times felt sorry for myself! It was so bad in my house I played with Barbies and I liked it! I like to shop. I love Adele. And I even sit down to go pee now. But I know that I love my daughters more than life itself. I am so proud of all of them and the strong, independent young ladies they have become. And with two granddaughters from our oldest Emily, (who is the BEST Mom) and her husband Ty, I have a feeling women will be part of my life for many more years to come. At least my son-in-law Ty and I will be joined by another man as my amazing daughter Madison will marry her fiancé James in the fall of 2016. They live in Denver and are loyal Broncos fans! My sweet Savanna is a twenty-two-year-old working college student and is one of the smartest people I know. Isabelle is a high school junior and it seems as if everyone she meets just instantly loves her sweet spirit. I just hope they understand how much I do love them.

Buddy and Jettie Gaines were the greatest parents a kid could ever ask for. They divorced when I was about six years old and remained friends. When my dad and his incredible wife of thirty years, Laurie, come to Winter Haven to visit my sister Tracy, they stay at my mom's house. My parents supported me wholeheartedly but two examples stand out. One is encouragement. Whenever I failed at something they were both there to offer that inspiration to try something else. The other is unconditional love. I knew whether I won a race or lost they would always be the same when I came back to them. It was something I could count on and there is no doubt that they each were so deserving of the two of my three gold medals I gave them after the Olympics. There is simply no way I can ever tell them how much they have meant to me as parents.

My sister, Tracy, and I didn't get along very much when we were kids. I picked on her quite a bit and we often fought like cats and dogs. Time and maturity tend to take care of that. Today, she is one of my best friends and someone I am so fortunate to be close to, though she likes to needle me that I didn't win four gold medals. She expected that one.

My grandparents were my heroes. I idolized all four of them and I have fond memories as a child being with them. Don't ever take your grandparents for granted. Please. There isn't a day that goes by that I don't think about my grandparents and cherish the short time I had with them.

My coaches have all been an instrumental part of my life.

Richard Quick was my mentor and my most trusted advisor. I would not have made the Olympic team, let alone win three gold medals, had it not been for Richard. He prepared me mentally and physically for the most perfect race I ever swam, and specifically gave me advice on my start that I know helped me win. I talk a lot more about Richard in the book. More than anything, though, Richard was a person I could talk to outside of the pool about my everyday struggles. Richard was diagnosed with an inoperable brain tumor on Christmas Eve, 2008. Six months later he was gone. I think about him all the time and I miss him so very much.

Eddie Reese took a chance on a skinny hick from a small town in Florida and for that I will forever be indebted to him. He recruited me when no one else did. He called me throughout my senior year in high school. He personally came to watch me swim in my state championship. When he left Auburn after my freshman year to become the head coach at Texas it was a difficult decision to stay. I wanted to follow Eddie. However, I also felt it was best for me to remain at an institution where I was growing from a boy to a man. Of course, I ended up swimming under the greatest coach on earth, Richard Quick. I am an Auburn man and always will be.

There have been many other coaches who have offered

guidance and mentorship...Bill Woolwine (my high school coach), Sam Griner, Doc Counsilman, Kris Kubik, David Marsh, John Asmuth, and Don Gambril. I share my triumphs with them as well.

I also want to thank Dainon Moody, the author of Rowdy Rising. I have been approached many times over the years to write a book about my life but never felt the timing was right. Dainon and I worked at The Limu Company and became good friends along the way. He came to me one day and said, "Let's put your story into words (or maybe I went to him). Either way, we have formed a bond and he has encapsulated my journey.

Mary Shanklin is the publisher and editor of my book. She is one of the brightest people I have ever met and I instantly trusted her when we met. She has added the perfect touch to help Dainon and me and without her Rowdy Rising would not have happened.

If anyone had told me that I would be broadcasting my seventh Olympic Games in Rio I would have told them they were crazy. My broadcasting career has been longer than my swimming career was. And there are so many people who have impacted that side of my life. John Naber taught me everything about being a broadcaster and to learn from one of my heroes of the 1976 Olympic team was even more special. And I know I would not be doing this trade for thirty years without the mentorship, patience and especially the friendship of Dan Hicks. He is the ultimate professional and I am so lucky to be calling my sixth Games with him in Rio (I called my first with Jim Donovan). I've called races with dozens of other play by play pros and all have been great experiences. But beside John and Dan some do stand out like my pals Ted Robinson and Craig Hummer, two amazing colleagues and so good at what they do.

Behind the scenes in a broadcast is where all the work is done. The production teams are the real heroes when it comes to what you see on the screen. I have done most of my work with the incredible producer (and director) Peter Lasser. He has produced virtually every swimming event the last ten to fifteen years and I cannot begin to thank him enough for his ultimate professionalism and friendship. Tommy Roy will be our producer on the Olympics for the fourth time in Rio and there's a reason why. No one comes as prepared for his craft more than Tommy. I sit in amazement when I watch him and director Drew Esocoff work thirty cameras and manage a hundred people all like a Leonard Bernstein or John Williams —simply incredible. Josh Freedenberg, Paul Bronsteader, Larry Herr, Mark Wolff and Mike Unger have all been terrific to work with over the years as well.

From my childhood chums who I am still close to today like Ralph Enzor, Jeb Fields, and Drew Ireland to ones who came later I have been blessed. Dru Dunworth, David Marsh, Rob Butcher and Mike Unger are the four most marvelous men I have ever met. All are incredibly successful in their own right and they have all been such huge mentors of mine and guys I have always been able to count on through all the peaks and valleys in so many areas of my life over the last thirty years or so. Janet Evans, Dick Carson, Bud Greenspan, Harris Rosen, Brett Hawke have been there as well.

Family friends like the Burlinghams, the Masters, the Andersons, the Meisenheimers, the Flanagan family, and my wife's family the Zacheas have been "family" to the Gaineses for years and years.

My management team over the years is a big reason for my longevity in the sport. From Parkes Brittain, the agent I signed with in the summer of 1983 (I was the first swimmer to ever sign with an agent and Parkes was an incredible innovator) to Evan Morgenstein to my current management family Chicago Sports Partners I have been blessed with people who care about me and the sport.

It was an honor to work for USA Swimming for many years and Chuck Weilgus, was and still is the executive director. He is such an awe-inspiring leader and I learned from him the meaning of "under promise and over deliver." Most of all he has always shown his genuine love of his fellow man through a remarkable selflessness even when he has been dealt a tough hand with cancer.

I have been with The Limu Company as a spokesperson and brand ambassador for over eleven years. The Founder, President and CEO, Gary Raser has been an example of perseverance and determination to me since I met him. He created a thriving company that changes people's lives with a fabulous product. He is an uncommonly generous man and I have learned so much from his leadership skills. Judy and I are very fortunate to have the Raser family in our lives.

My new position is at the YMCA of Central Florida as Vice President of Aquatics. I am thrilled to work under Dan Wilcox, our President and CEO. Dan has been a Y man for thirty two years. His depth of experience and passion for the Y cause is contagious for all of us who work at the Y. I am so excited about where our organization is heading and the lives we will be impacting under Dan's leadership.

As I head into the twilight of my professional career I get to do what I love every single day. My office is ten feet from the pool, and with thirty six pools, I have quite the "office." More importantly we are impacting families all the time. Our mission is simple: to improve lives of all in Central Florida by connecting individuals, families and communities with opportunities based on Christian values that strengthen Spirit, Mind and Body.

Of course I think that mission is done through aquatics. And if it has anything to do with water we have the program. I am most proud of our Safe Start initiative. With Florida leading the nation in the number of childhood drowning deaths, the Y along with our phenomenal partner Dr. Phillips Charities have Safe Start which is our groundbreaking infant water survival program. Since 1999, more than 13,400 local children have learned how to be safer, secure and confident around water thanks to Safe Start.

I have worked for or served as an ambassador to The USA Swimming Foundation for the past thirteen years. Our mission has always been simple: to raise funds and support programs that save lives and build champions in the pool and in life.

I feel the same way about the ZAC Foundation, which I have been with the last four years. Motivated by a mission of love, Brian and Karen Cohn created the ZAC Foundation as a living legacy to their son Zachary who tragically drowned at age five. In his name, the ZAC Foundation is working to ensure that never again will a child suffer the same heart-rending fate. It seeks to create a generational change in how water safety is viewed by parents and their children and I am so proud to be a small part of this journey with them.

We will one day stop childhood drowning and I know The Central Florida YMCA, USA Swimming Foundation and the ZAC Foundation will all have a part in it.

It has been an honor to serve as an advocate for Swim Across America for thirty years. Everyone has been affected by cancer. It is certainly personal for me. I lost my step-father and step-sister to cancer. My father has battled cancer. My sister-in-law is now battling cancer. With the help of hundreds of volunteers nationwide, and past and current Olympians, Swim Across America is helping find a cure for cancer. I know with the new leadership by my dear friend Rob Butcher, SAA will continue to being a force in helping to find a cure for cancer.

All four charitable organizations that have meant the most to me over the years: The Central Florida YMCA, The USA Swimming Foundation, Swim Across America, and the ZAC Foundation will share in the proceeds of Rowdy Rising's sales.

There will be no Ambrose Gaines the fifth. With four daughters and no sons that ship has sailed. But I know in my heart that there will be many Gaineses in the future, who will read this book and know a lot more about someone who was admittedly an underdog and came out on top in so many more ways than one. There will be names I have forgotten to thank but I hope they all know how much they have impacted my life. Enjoy Rowdy Rising!

— Rowdy Gaines

TABLE OF CONTENTS

Rowdy Rising

From Rejected to Unrivaled

by Dainon Moody

Olympian Turned Lifeguard

Perched atop his lifeguard chair, Ambrose "Rowdy" Gaines IV looked out at the Lake Region Country Club pool filled with playing children and watchful adults sunning themselves on a warm July day in 1980. He was there, but his thoughts were in another place altogether. As children played Marco Polo, Gaines contemplated another pool, one thousands of miles away from the humidity of Central Florida.

At just twenty years of age, the ten-time world record holder and five-time NCAA champion thought about the Luzhniki Sports Complex pool in Moscow, Russia. He'd never set foot in its waters, but couldn't stop wondering what it might have been like. What if he had been there when a team of Soviet swimmers dominated the 1980 Olympics? How might that have gone differently? These were the very Games that would have defined his entire life. That was where

Olympic Gold Medalist Sergei Kopliakov failed to beat his own world-record time while Rowdy, who could swim faster than the Russian, now guarded sunbathers and children splashing in the water.

When President Jimmy Carter pushed through a boycott of the 1980 Games – the result of the Soviet invasion of Afghanistan–it came as a shock to Rowdy and hundreds of world-class athletes from the United States and the rest of the world. The Carter administration had been moving toward a boycott but few fully expected it. Even in speaking to a group of American athletes intent on competing in Moscow, Carter admitted having "some degree of trepidation."

Ultimately, the Cold War opponents boycotted each other's Games. To say it was a disappointing time to be a competitive swimmer may be one of the bigger understatements of Rowdy's storied career. He'd devoted himself to swimming in high school and college, making and breaking world records with increasing regularity, constantly shaving seconds off his times all along the way. He'd been favored to win as many as five gold medals. What was to be a pinnacle achievement for him and for the entire nation was laid to waste with the Cold War standoff.

Competing in the Olympics had been a destiny he had been robbed of. Rowdy – along with the rest of the American Olympians wanting desperately to compete — had hit a dead end of global proportions. Pentathlete Jane Frederick has since told historic scholars her thoughts at the time: "Today, I'm being exposed to the iron realities of the world." Olympic gymnastics hopeful Debbie Landreth trained five years for the lost Games of 1980. Once her nation boycotted, she said there was an "empty feeling to be unable to fulfill [her] goals."

Their dreams had been eliminated. For athletes so used to making the impossible possible, this was an all-new kind of roadblock.

Decades later and far removed from the Winter Haven pool of Rowdy's youth, that same crushing disappointment still haunts him: "My first reaction wasn't shock. It was anger. I was angry at my country and angry at Carter specifically.

"Over time, that anger turned into pity, self-pity. I started feeling sorry for myself and thought my career was over with. A feeling of helplessness followed that. I thought for sure, for me at least, this was the beginning of the end."

And that's something few consider. Unconquerable Olympian-trained athletes are ultimately just as human as those not attempting to attach their names to a gold medal.

Rowdy was defeated before he began. Instead of weighing his

options, he took the way out that no one expected: The world's fastest swimmer and distinguished Auburn University graduate bowed out completely. Which is to say he promptly retired early, taking up a job as a lifeguard.

"And, believe me, you have a lot of time to think when you're just sitting in a high chair, watching kids running around all day," he recalls, letting on he constantly wondered whether or not he'd done the right thing. His decision to retire from swimming dogged him constantly for six long months. It did more harm than good; that time in his life became increasingly empty for him.

When most people his age were filling up their days with dating, textbooks, jobs and parties, his was a world of lament. Rowdy feared his views on the Olympic movement had soured. Had he been allowed to compete, he was favored to win big and return a national hero, even an inspiration for other budding athletes. Now he found himself wondering if any of that was ever going to happen at all, if he'd ever be allowed to see how far he could get in his sport on a worldwide level. Would he really want to give up another four years of his life training only to have the Games canceled all over again? In his mind, that was the possibility.

The summer Rowdy started working as a lifeguard in his

hometown, he was reminded over and over of the Olympics. The lost opportunity flooded his life when he'd see the famous rings on television and when he'd drive past the Olympic billboards flanking the highway. The sights gutted him. Every time he'd get that reminder, he'd get a pang in his chest, like he'd been hit square in the ribs with a softball. On the day his arch international rivals competed in the event he dominated – the 200 Freestyle – he sat on his lifeguard's chair in uncomfortable anticipation. There was no nearby television broadcasting the event, just occasional highlights. He told Lakeland Ledger Sports Columnist Mike Cobb: "I knew the results came in around five, but I didn't want to call and find out. I just didn't want to know."

His suffering was apparent to all around him, maybe most of all to his own parents. It was his father, Ambrose "Buddy" Gaines III, who came in and helped steer his only son. The words he chose not only served to redirect Rowdy, they inspired a change that would alter the course of Olympic history. What he said to his son, Rowdy took to heart.

"My dad was really cool. He said, 'You know, it's not going to affect me one way or the other if you choose to swim in the Olympics or not. But what you choose will affect you for the rest of your life, not knowing if you could have made it. It's four years out of your life, but you have fifty more ahead of you."

That single piece of advice was what Rowdy needed to hear. It's what got him off his lifeguard chair and back into the pool.

"It changed everything for me," he says, noting it was the reason he decided to finally go for it. "I felt like, if I didn't, I'd have had to look in the mirror and say 'what if' for a long, long time."

He'd already trained for the Olympics for four years and understood he would have to double that amount while training for the 1984 Games. He knew he would be older than those he was swimming against, stars in their own right competing at their peak level performance. But he was able to draw on his experience swimming long before Moscow had even been on the horizon. He'd carved out a reputation for himself by doing all he'd done in the pool. One might say all the various events of his life had led to this moment.

Years later, Buddy recalls the pivotal conversation with his son. While he's quick to refuse any credit for getting Rowdy to reconsider his choice, he does remember giving him what amounted to a piece of his mind, a good portion of that sometimes-requisite tough love.

Sitting on the back porch of his Little Gasparilla Island Florida beach home and looking out on seemingly endless Gulf waters, his father recounts the pivotal talk.

"I said, 'You're going to be a ding dong if you don't try again,'" he said. "In 1984, you're going to ask yourself, 'Why didn't I keep swimming?' and you're going to feel terrible.

"So Rowdy hung out for a year and I just said 'Don't do it. Please don't do it. You'll hate yourself for it.' And he was very nervous and they called him a has-been and Muhammad Ali and all sorts of bad names once he actually started competing again."

Among the naysayers was *Chicago Sun-Times* sports columnist Ray Sons. He called Rowdy a retread and "member of the Lost Generation of American Olympians of 1980."

Buddy said his son did far more than just prove them wrong: "They said he'd never cut the mustard, but he came back and he murdered them. Just killed them."

And so began the real journey of Rowdy Gaines, the man who was born to swim, sometimes to win gold medals, sometimes to break world records and always to inspire those who watched him.

He came to understand that, when it came to his life, it was best lived competing in the water. That's something he knew all along. It just took him a while to come to terms with that.

"In the back of my mind, I suppose I always felt like I was going to go for it," he says. "I was never going to give up, not entirely. I felt like I had to do this. It was always gnawing at me. I just needed to get over the hump mentally.

"I'd swum so long already. I just couldn't give up. Not then. Not now."

Postscript

If I thought I would have had 1980 and done what I was supposed to have done, my [expected] times would have won five gold medals. I was ranked first in the world and would have been on three relays. If that had happened, I probably would not have swum in 1984.

I came out of this whole ordeal smelling like a rose. I had '84, I had Los Angeles, I got to compete on American soil and was a part of the first commercial Olympics. It's almost a guilt feeling now, when you think that there were 363 athletes on that 1980 team who didn't make it in 1976 or 1984. That was the one shot they had. So they never had a chance to compete. I feel for them. They are all heroes in my book.

An athlete's life can come and go in the span of four years. And, in eight years, that's a lifetime. The person that best exemplifies the 1980 boycott for me is Craig Beardsley. Think about it. In 1980, he would have won the gold medal by two seconds. I just feel bad for him. He trained four more years, just like I did, and he got third at our trials in 1984. And he didn't make it."

Setbacks come in all shapes and sizes. Some are small and easily overcome and there are some that seem completely insurmountable. With the boycott, there was just no way you could have done anything about what happened at that moment.

Still, whatever the setback is, you should never give up on that goal of yours if it's still attainable. I've had so many different little setbacks here and there. That was the biggest setback I'd ever had in swimming, but I overcame it. As it turns out, I am living proof you should never give up. There's always a way to overcome.

I'm not saying the 363 athletes didn't have the will, but they didn't have the way. I worked the graveyard shift as a night clerk at a hotel. I lived on macaroni and cheese. I slept on the floor of a friend's apartment for a full year. I did what I had to do to survive. I'm not in their shoes, but, as far as my situation goes? I'm glad I wasn't 364th. I was bound and determined not to be. There was no other option. I put a lot of pressure on myself, but eight years is too long to work for something and not get it. That wasn't going to happen for me.

— Rowdy Gaines

The best thing that ever happened to Rowdy was what Carter did, because it ended up defining who he is. And he's such an amazing ambassador for swimming. What politics took away, he'd been allowed to give back by making the sport better.

And three gold medals in 1984 is a much bigger story than if he'd won five in 1980.

If he'd have won five, he would have retired and he'd not be swimming today.

The struggles defined his appreciation for swimming. Yes, he was deeply affected, but those are the moments that end up defining us. Swimming has no idea how we were indirectly affected by that happening. It wasn't great for all involved, but it helped define who Rowdy was and is.

– Dru Dunworth, longtime friend

Playing with Gators

Rowdy's mom, Jettie, is a former professional water skier still living in Polk County, near where she raised her children in Winter Haven, Florida. She remembers her son's first experience with water and what it meant for him. Having almost single-handedly raised her son near various shorelines of a myriad of lakes all during the formative years of his life, she's quick to confirm he learned to swim before he could walk. He was nine months old and crawling across Lake Eloise's sandy beach one day when she decided to give him a bit of a nudge in the right direction.

The earliest glimpses of Rowdy's love for water and his talent at propelling himself through it started with Jettie putting a Styrofoam bubble of sorts on her son's back, one that attached with a belt. The mother of two said there simply was no other gear for infants who had any inclinations to swim, at least not at the time. She made do with what she had.

From that point on, however, she had to improvise.

"Little by little, I started cutting pieces of it off until, pretty soon, nothing was left but the belt itself," she recalls. Just like that, her boy was off and swimming. Rowdy was on his way.

Her motivation for teaching him was easy to understand, too: Jettie wanted to save his life. After all, the lake they lived on was all of fifteen feet from their front door and she didn't much care to leave that kind of thing to chance. So she helped teach Rowdy what she knew about swimming. She did the same with his younger sister, Tracy, who would go on to snag a spot on her swim team when she was barely out of kindergarten. If nothing else, teaching her children to swim and love the water allowed her some peace of mind for those times she didn't happen to have an eye on them.

The more you learn about Rowdy's childhood, the more you realize much of his training began by simply playing in the water in lakes. Doing so allowed his passion to develop. Contrast that with future competitors refining their strokes in juniors programs and camps and you quickly realize spending time actually playing versus being drilled with instruction isn't such a bad thing.

She never says so outright, but it stands to reason that Rowdy's mom was some kind of influence on his love for water and being in it. After all, she had traveled all the way from her native Mississippi to become what they called an "Aqua Maid" at Cypress

Gardens, once known as the Water Ski Capital of the World and located in Winter Haven. At that time, she was all but determined to water ski and perform for her daily bread. She had such a strong desire to do so, in fact, she abandoned her college education at Mississippi State College after one year to follow her heart; she was absolutely convinced it was where she needed to be.

And she loved it, she really did. To hear her talk about it today — to hear her recall the life that was so far removed from her current one — is to hear why she can't help but smile at the remembrance.

Rowdy's mom and the rest of the skiers performed in thirty-minute shows four times a day. She lived that life for several years. As one of the taller skiers, she ended up at the bottom of the water skier pyramid most of the time. It probably led to the back problems she still has now, but she doesn't so much focus on that.

"There was ski jumping, a clown act and even a ballet where we wore tutus," she says, "where we'd be on one ski and hold a rope on our heel. Oh, it was a marvelous time."

And Rowdy, who started tackling strokes before he took his first baby steps, would go on to learn how to water ski at the age of four. It was easy to tell he had a clear love for being in the water, whether he was skiing or swimming in it. If told he needed to leave the lake at any given time and get back inside the house, he'd get around to doing so, but not right away, never right away. But eventually. He'd take that longest way around, whatever it happened to be.

It wasn't so much his fault as he just couldn't help himself.

"I just always felt more comfortable in the water than I did on land," he's quick to say. "I would always be in it. And when I wasn't, I wanted to be. Water was a large part of my parents' lives — Cypress Gardens was how and where they met — and it was part of my grandparents' lives before them. They lived on the lake as well. It tied all of us together."

His dad was a photographer at the park, though he did a lot of other things on his way to getting there. Still, whether he was taking photos or driving around the boat that pulled the skiers, he was a true fixture of Cypress Gardens. And it was the nine-to-five of their somewhat unorthodox occupations that eventually brought Rowdy's parents together.

For his first seventeen years, Rowdy lived next to at least one lake. They pretty much ran the gamut. They were clear, clean, deep, small, oblong and a lot of other things in between. Lake Eloise was round, about a mile wide, and too large to swim all the way to the bottom.

Rowdy and his sister, Tracy, learned to swim at an early age.

His mom is quick to point out that living so near the water wasn't the kind of status symbol then that it tends to be today: It just was what it was. At one point, there were only two houses on Lake Eloise. One belonged to his folks and the other to his grandparents. And the lake became his playground, jungle gym, backyard and sandbox all rolled into one. It was their reality.

So was his taking the boat out when he was all of eight years old. It was having his brother-in-law build a ski ramp out of plywood and Styrofoam, waxing it up real nice, positioning it in the lake's middle, attaching some weights to hold it in place and allowing everyone to use it as a sort of makeshift water slide. Those realities involved sneaking into a swimming pool shaped like the state of Florida for as long as he and his friends could get away with before getting caught (and they always got caught). And since it was the Sunshine State, playing in the lake occasionally meant chasing and catching alligators when the situation presented itself. And it did – frequently.

Rowdy and his cousins occasionally spent their afternoons swimming right into gator nests, scaring mama off, catching a few of her babies and rolling them over on their backs. They were as fearless as the gators were fearful. It was as safe as catching a big lizard or turtle, at least in their eyes. They didn't know any differently. Little known fact: Rubbing an alligator on its belly will actually cause it to fall asleep and get completely paralyzed for fifteen seconds or so. For Rowdy, that may have been the most fun part of it all. It was why they did what they did.

Of course gators can be a deadly proposition. While over 1.3 million alligators live in Florida and can be found in each of its sixty-seven counties, they generally shy away from humans and only get aggressive if they feel threatened. Since the 1940s, there have been about a dozen attacks documented yearly, and about twenty from the last forty years or more have been fatal.

Not that Rowdy knew much about those kinds of statistics at the time.

"We weren't gator wrestlers or anything, I wouldn't go that far," he quickly points out, saying he'd never even think about tackling an alligator more than half his size. "It was just fun for us. And it's not like we fed them either. Tourists feed them all the time now, so gators have lost all fear."

In the Winter Haven of his youth, capturing an alligator was akin to having a stray cat follow you home. His mom tells of a time when they made the mistake of keeping one of the alligators on as a pet, something that was never repeated in their house ever again, and for good reason. It got to be about three feet long – even earning a name everyone seems to have forgotten – before they decided to release it back to the lake.

Jettie: "Rowdy put him in a baby pool and they had him a

while. But that gator started hissing, biting and slapping his tail at them, so we had to let it go. As I said before, they're mean. Real mean."

If at first you don't succeed, fail, fail again

Part of Rowdy's story, something that gets shared when he talks about what propelled him forward, is that he managed to get cut from five different sports teams before he ever found one that wanted to keep him. Swimming wasn't part of the plan as much as it was something that happened. It's testament to his desire to keep trying, as many times as it took to get to where he wanted to be. Being cut from the teams may even be putting it all too nicely: He never made it past tryouts.

It's a funny thing, but the sport that would soon define him barely managed to make it onto his list of possibilities when he was attending Winter Haven High School. Football, on the other hand, was his first stab at high-school stardom. There was one reason alone he wanted to wear the school's Blue Devils football uniform: It was all about girls.

"My pea-brained tenth-grade mind would say that football players got all the chicks," he says. He thought making the team would make him more attractive, even allow him to fit in with his peers. Instead, he lasted just two days.

"That didn't work out. So I went on to basketball, then to baseball. Nothing. I had zero talent. I didn't make a single one of the teams."

According to him, there was a reason nothing was taking. Maybe it was the fact he really didn't have any talent (something his dad is quick to take issue with). But, secondly, there was his physique to consider. He was all of five feet nine and twenty three pounds (give or take a hundred).

"They could blow on me and I'd fall down," he says, still sounding exasperated these more than forty years later.

After trying out for team after team and remaining ever consistent at his ability to fail, the time came for swim team tryouts. It was the next to last sport he'd try, simply because he was running out of options. Rowdy was so certain he wouldn't make it, he was in the library researching track and field events he could try out for once he received that expected news. He didn't even know those events, but he was going to tackle them. He knew running was one — and he hated to run — really, truly hated it. But he'd do that if he had to. Something was sure to stick.

"I was going to skip over swimming entirely. It was one of those things I took for granted, something I could play with and enjoy, but not a sport I wanted to work very hard at," Rowdy says. "It wasn't even a sport to me growing up. It was just something we did. Pure recreation."

He credits childhood best friend Bobby Vaughn for helping get him interested in the first place. Initially, it was just Bobby who wanted to try out for the swim team. Born legally blind – completely unable to see out of one eye and only able to see 25 percent of the world with his other – Bobby felt swimming was the one sport he could succeed at. He didn't need perfect vision to make the team; he just needed to get properly trained. Fortunately, Rowdy offered his help. He was swimming laps right next to him for months, helping Bobby make his turns and making certain he didn't hit his head. The two friends got in such good shape in the process, Rowdy changed his mind about trying out.

The seemingly impossible happened: He made the team, his first. (As did Bobby.) The coach was willing to give him a shot. It caused his world and the way he saw it – as well as how he regarded swimming—to shift, and considerably so.

It did, however, take some getting used to. The pool was not very glamorous. It was a fifteen-minute drive from the school and located in the middle of Florence Villa. The pool was kept up well enough, but it was unheated. And, when practice started in February, it was far too cold for a teenager who didn't have any body fat to insulate him.

"To this day, I don't know how I lasted," he says. "I don't know why I didn't quit."

Rowdy rising

"Rowdy" wasn't the name on his birth certificate, though it's a nickname that's never gone away. His real name is Ambrose Gaines IV, the name passed down to him by his father, who got the name from his father. And that's not where that name originated, even. In fact, there are six or so men in his history who have answered to the name Ambrose over the years.

But, since he was five, the world has been happy with switching out Ambrose for Rowdy, no matter what the situation. Not that Rowdy was doing any complaining. The name he'd been given just wasn't very popular in the classroom.

He explains: "Think about it, what would you rather be called? Ambrose or Rowdy? I'm proud of the name Ambrose now. But it was a tough name for me to grow up with. Rowdy, on the other hand, wasn't anywhere. When my name was called on the first day of school, I would hear my teacher say: 'Ambrose? Ambrose Gaines? Can I see Ambrose Gaines the Fourth please?' It's no wonder I got bullied."

Adding a number after his name seemed to make matters worse.

"Rowdy Gaines the Fourth ... now, isn't that pompous?" Jettie says. "We didn't want to call him Buddy or Little Buddy or any of that stuff. So, from the beginning, he was Rowdy. And he and his father are the only Ambroses left."

Reporters through the years couldn't resist having fun with the polar opposite names.

A writer for the *New York Times* wrote in April 1979: "His name is Ambrose Gaines 4th and he is not a Wall Street lawyer, an investment broker, or owner of an America's Cup yacht. He is a swimmer and tonight he won the men's 200-meter freestyle in what could have been the strongest field in history."

The local press in Winter Haven also enjoyed playing off his name on Jan. 5, 1981: "Rowdy Gaines, a guy with a name like a tag-team wrestler, spent the weekend destroying a couple of myths about competitive swimming."

And a headline on a 1980 piece by *Phoenix Gazette* Sports Columnist Larry Ward read: "Well, Rowdy's Better Than Ambrose, What?"

Originally borrowed from Clint Eastwood's Rowdy Yates character in *Rawhide*, Rowdy was a nickname his parents both agreed on.

"He was a really cool character in the show, so we gave him the nickname. It's so hokey, too, because Rowdy is anything but rowdy," his dad said.

Apparently his coach at Auburn agreed. In recognizing his swim team captain for the school's prestigious Cliff Hare Award in 1981, Coach Richard Quick described him as the team's spiritual leader: "He is a man of great character, great leadership and great understanding."

Postscript

When you go through those valleys, especially in your younger years, it really helps to know the weight of the world is not on your shoulders. Those disappointments are tough to handle. It's why we rely on others for support. I had solid friendships. I had a family structure that was positive."

It forces you to learn a lot about yourself. As I faced those adversities, as I fell further and further down the foxhole, I'd start questioning things. At the same time, I started relying more on those around me. They'd get me through. You don't have to do these things yourself. You should go to others for support, especially the people you believe in. You end up believing they believe in you, too."

I never got too discouraged. Even after the fourth and fifth times I didn't make the team. I didn't throw my arms up and say forget this. I always felt like tomorrow was another day."

And you do feel alone in your teen years. I still tell teenagers it's never too late to achieve their dreams. I look a 15-year-old kid in the eye and if I see hopelessness, I try to give him hope."

The people around me said, 'Hey, maybe

football's not your bag, but why not the baseball team? Why not tennis or golf?' My parents were good at nudging me, but they never shoved me. There was no pressure. There was always that patience."

The most successful people I know have always been able to live through the peaks but it's their valleys they're defined by. The times I lost or failed, I learned more about how to succeed the next time. I got a little better and lasted a little longer. Each time I figured more out about what it took."

—Rowdy Gaines

Finding the Magic

Swimming fast became Rowdy's way of getting to where he wanted to be. As would happen so many times for him later in life, he soon discovered that winning race after race would open some very big doors and opportunities for him — to the tune of landing him in college, if he wanted it. And, the truth is, he wanted it badly. While it was never necessarily expected of him, he was afraid of where his life might end up if he didn't go. Maybe, just maybe, he could be actually be good enough at swimming to earn a scholarship.

As neither he nor his parents had the money to enroll him even if he wanted to go, Rowdy soon learned how far winning could take him. Only, it didn't start out that way. When he started on the swim team his junior year of high school, he just didn't feel like he was very good.

In fact, at the state swim meet during the spring of his junior year, Rowdy had finished fifteenth out of sixteen in the boys' 100-yard freestyle. He later told a reporter for the Winter Haven newspaper: "After doing so badly, I told myself that I'm never going to do that again. I made such a fool of myself and I was determined to do better when I got back there."

The budding athlete spent the summer before his senior year, and most of the school year, developing his stroke.

When someone from Auburn University showed up, saw him swimming at a meet and thought enough about what he'd seen to go back and alert the coach, that gave Rowdy a boost. Not only did it mean there might be a future for him in the sport, it was a turning point as well: Someone outside of his friends and family believed in what it was he could do.

"What [David McCagg of Auburn] saw in me was the big picture: He saw potential," Rowdy says. "My stroke was pretty raw, but it was mechanically sound considering I'd only been swimming for six months." At the time, he rode high on the water, had a high elbow catch and hadn't even gone through a growth spurt yet, so he was just going to get bigger, stronger and — fingers crossed — faster.

The Auburn camp coaches offered up their share of positive observations, like the fact he was so light on the water. They were also glad he hadn't swum competitively or bothered with weight training; it meant he had the opportunity to improve once he came into his own in college. In essence, they saw a potentially bright future for the swimmer. They could see he had certain characteristics even he couldn't see in himself at the time: They looked past what was right in front of them at what could and would be, given the right amount of determination and effort.

Because it was his first full year swimming, Rowdy didn't know what exactly what he wanted out of it. He did know he had found his passion; he was going to try his hardest to be good at it. That meant not just dedicating himself not just in the pool, but outside it as well. That summer, he checked out all the library books he could find about swimming from his local library, poring over books like Sherm Chavoor's *The 50-Meter Jungle: How Olympic Gold Swimmers are Made* and Don Schollander's *Deep Water*.

He did so because he wanted to get better. And, as far as he was concerned, that meant learning the history of the sport. In his mind, if he studied it from a technical and historical standpoint, he couldn't help but improve.

The Olympics weren't even a goal for him, not yet, but getting a full scholarship certainly was. Rowdy wasn't sure he'd be able to go to college otherwise. And so he decided early on that he would go to the school offering him the most money. He started down that road by writing personal letters to every college he could think of. He dropped off fifty letters to fifty universities at the post office, each with the words "Swim Coach" across the envelopes where names would normally be.

"And all the letters said pretty much the same thing," he says. "I told them my name and my times and I'd ask them, 'How fast do I have to go to get a scholarship to your school?'"

Even *Lakeland Ledger* sports writer Bob McClure wrote during Spring 1977: "Rowdy Gaines, who swims for the Winter Haven swim team, wants to go to college. He knows the only way he's going to accomplish the goal is to get a scholarship."

Ultimately, swim coaches and universities across the nation started responding.

He confirms: "They started recruiting me before my senior year even started. Now, I wasn't any good, so that meant something. Auburn had a good swim team already. The coach there, Eddie Reese, saw something in me. He always had an eye for talent. Still does."

There are more than a few reasons Eddie is considered one of the best swim coaches in the world, but it largely comes down to how he would analyze talent in a way few others did. Medals and awards weren't as necessary to him as viewing the person from all sides. He wanted to know how a swimmer felt the water, how comfortable they were in it. Was he fast as a twelve-year-old only to have plateaued near the end of his high school career? Or was he part of a steady projection and headed straight up?

At Auburn, Eddie had taken a very young team – most of whom had been "no names" in high school – and created something that elevated the collective into the realm of spectacular. They were sixth in the nation when Rowdy was a senior at Winter Haven. They catapulted to second when he started as a freshman. Eddie had essentially handpicked novices and turned them into superstars.

Little by little, Rowdy inched forward in his progress, shaving whole seconds off his time. He learned how spending more time in the pool and disciplining his body would pay off – more time there led to more speed.

In his junior year, he could only last forty-five minutes of back-and-forth laps before becoming totally fatigued. So Winter Haven Swim Coach Bill Woolwine suggested he do doubles (two practices per day) even when nobody else on the team was doing so. The more he swam, the more his desire to improve increased. He got stronger and bigger. His stroke got better. And, by his senior year, Rowdy Gaines was untouchable: He was easily managing two hours or more of pool time a day.

By the time Rowdy swam in the state championships his senior year, he still didn't feel like he had proven himself. He'd worked all year doing all kinds of things in the water and knew he was about to improve at the exact right time. To this day, all competitive teenage swimmers strive to do what it was he wanted to do, too: Head out of high school on the highest possible note.

"Did I know exactly what I was doing? I had no idea," Rowdy remembers. "But from what I'd read and from conversations I'd had with swimmers better than I was, I knew I was ready. I'd been setting myself up to peak."

As a final step in preparation for the championships, he did more than shave seconds off his best times. He and another swimmer on his team shaved all the hair off their heads with a straight razor — an act he'd later vow never to repeat. It took six full months for his hair to grow back to its normal length. Still, it helped illustrate his dedication. If shaving your head amounted to an increase in speed —

even if it was just a mental trick — he was all for it. He wanted to test it out.

Rowdy came through, both for himself and the growing crowd of supporters: He made drastic improvements on his times, dropping from 48 seconds in the 100 yards to 45 and from 1 minute 46 seconds in the 200 yards to a much faster 1 minute 41 seconds. Statistics like this are impressive all by themselves, but how impressive were they in 1977? Good enough to allow him not only to win his state championships, but to become the fifth fastest high school kid in the entire country just a year after he'd come in almost dead last at the same event.

When Rowdy touched the wall and won State, having swum faster than anybody else, the race he'd trained so hard for was over. But his mind was moving at a steady clip. He thought, maybe he was pretty good at this. Maybe he could do something bigger than a full-ride scholarship. Having arrived at this kind of position doing something he really loved doing — and especially after so many failures — there was an overwhelming sense of relief.

After clinching the state title, his cousin Jan rushed to him to give him a hug, as did his mom, dad and girlfriend. They all wrapped their arms around him and created what he remembers as a "cocoon of pure joy." Having tried so hard for so long to have something like this happen, to be this good at something he loved that much, it was an all-new sensation for him.

The local newspaper started off its story on the meet simply: "Rowdy Gaines did it."

His coach was quoted saying at the time: "In another twenty years of coaching, I'm not likely to ever have another one like him." He cited his swim team star not only for his hard work and talent but also for being able to endure physical pain beyond what most swimmers could handle.

The win was a game changer, maybe even the very thing he'd need to compete at the national – or even international – level. It took him from almost being either a "walk on" at Auburn or earning a half scholarship at Western Kentucky (another school he was seriously considering) to ultimately being offered a full scholarship at Auburn.

Winning State meant other shifts, too. It had the power to morph his personality altogether. By his own admission, he became the big man on campus and high school athlete of the year his senior year, achieving the kinds of accolades he could only dream about actually happening to him before. He even went so far as to date the homecoming queen. Not bad for a kid who used to hide from bullies in the bathroom.

"Being fifth in the country? It gave me more self-confidence, it really did," Rowdy says. "I didn't even have that before. I was failing at everything I tried. I was at a low point, but gradually I started getting better. I finally had confidence in who I was and who I was going to be. I mean, I was afraid I would end up pumping gas at a local gas station."

"Winning that meet made me believe I belonged and that maybe I could be really good, that maybe I should pursue an Olympic dream even."

The talking heads at Auburn started riddling him with ideas, asking about his goals and aspirations. They let on that, if he wanted it badly enough, the Olympics really were within his reach. That got his full attention.

"It's the first I'd heard anything like that. I'd been dreaming about it for a year, but now it was something I could reach out and start to touch. That carrot was at the end of the stick and I could almost grab it. Before, I could barely see it."

When he decided to pick a college, it was one of his easier decisions, especially because he felt a kind of allegiance to Auburn. It had a good swim team, a good coach, a town that completely revolved around the school and, what's more, he'd be able to easily skip home for Thanksgiving and Christmas. And so it went: Auburn was where he'd try to make a name for himself. If it happened anywhere, it would happen there.

Once there, he started to earn a reputation. As a freshman, he was ranked second in the 200- and 500-yard freestyles and third in the 100-yard free.

His coach, Eddie Reese, commented to Rowdy's hometown newspaper about the young Floridian on his team: "He has a couple of attributes that really help. For one, he's very good in practice. And for another, he never lets anyone by him. Like, he beats everyone we line him up against."

Soon he met Richard Quick, a coach who'd signed on at the end of his first year as a freshman. Eddie Reese had taken a job at the University of Texas, along with half the team. But Quick played such an important role in shaping Rowdy's early career that the athlete later gave him one of his gold medals (his father and mother got the others).

Quick became the one person to keep Rowdy from going off to Texas with everybody else. He was his anchor.

"I just fell in love with him," he says. "I loved his energy, attitude, commitment, enthusiasm. We called him the 'Smiling Cobra' because he always had a big smile on his face when he walked in the room. In the water, though, he was a snake. He killed us. The smile stayed but he'd strike once we got in the water."

Auburn Coach Richard Quick congratulates Rowdy.

Case in point: Quick would have his team swim four lengths of the pool every minute and five seconds. If they hit that goal, he'd give them less time to complete the task, and so on. He never made their practices impossible, but he did make his team stretch towards success, setting and resetting goals all along the way.

For Rowdy, the reward for anything he accomplished was relatively simple: He yearned for approval. If he earned a "great job" from Quick, that's all he needed to go on. The pat on the head, the slap on the back, even a simple "nice swim" would energize him. When he swam, he'd look first to see if Quick was watching and, as long as he was, he swam better.

"He became my second father. Not the father I never had or anything, but I ended up living with him and his family one summer. It was a great relationship we started and I could feel the connection instantly," Rowdy says. He was the one coach responsible for his success. He was the one with Rowdy the longest, the one who saw him through many ups and downs.

Rowdy continued improving on his times, going from 1 minute 41 seconds to 1 minute 37 seconds in the 200 Free and shaving 2 seconds off his 100, both fairly dramatic changes. And, perhaps the biggest shift for the one-time skinny high schooler with so few muscles to speak of, he grew up. He filled out. He went from being five feet nine and 120 pounds to six feet one and 150. The growth spurt hit and launched him even further in the direction he wanted.

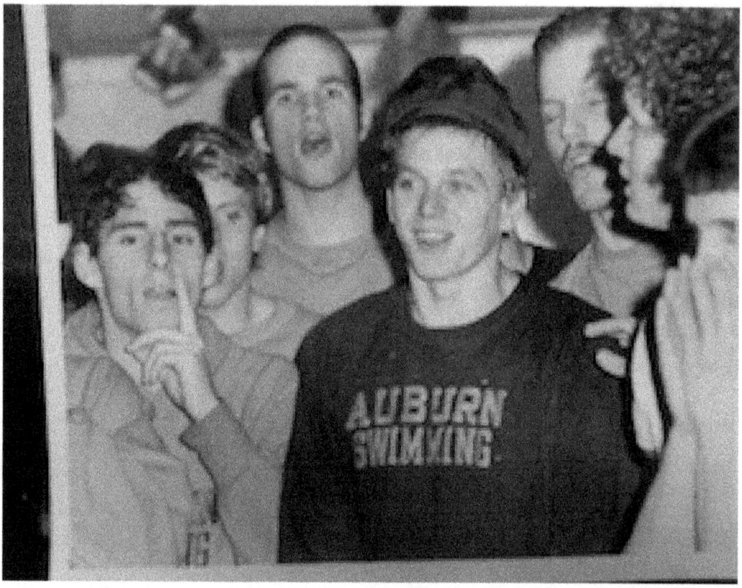

Rowdy and teammates at Auburn University.

The team at Auburn was filled with stars. There was David McCagg, the national champion on the team and Billy Forrester, a sophomore who was an Olympic bronze medalist in the 200-meter butterfly. Rowdy remembers him for never using goggles when he'd swim; he compared his former teammate to a "bull in the water." There was Scott Spann, too, another national champion who was built like a Greek god. These were the sorts he had read about in Swimming World magazine, making it intimidating and inspiring for him, all at once. Rowdy wanted to be like them; he wanted everything they had. And so he stuck as close to them as he could. He was their shadow, asking questions and hopeful some of their magic might rub off. He wanted to be around them every minute of the day.

Luckily — or perhaps as a direct result of his determination — he did gain some of that magic stuff. When it started happening and he really started to win, it wasn't just once. He won a second, a third and more. It became more habitual than happenstance. And by his sophomore year, even though they were all a class ahead of him, he was training harder than anyone else on the team.

At the time, his coach commented to the media: "He's almost the perfect individual to coach. He's sensitive. He's the newest star on the scene. He's the type of guy you'd like to see your son grow to be."

There were the NCAA Championships, when he came away with winning third in the 200 Free. There was the 100 Free, which had him coming out of the race recognized as the eighth-best in the whole country.

In just two years' time, from May of 1976 to March of 1978,

Rowdy Gaines went from virtually last in the 100 Free to winning the state championship and being the fifth fastest high school swimmer in the country. The next year, he was the third fastest. And, that summer, he made the world championships and finished second in the entire world.

He helps put that in an altogether different way: "I went from walking on the deck with a wet suit and not knowing how to do a flip turn to being second in the world in 30 months' time."

Postscript

One of the first swim camps we did at Auburn, maybe fifteen years ago, there was a young boy about fifteen years old who came up to me, and he had tears in his eyes when he told me how he was from a small school and was a swimmer. To make a long story short, he got bullied by another athlete on the baseball team, who told him swimming wasn't a sport and made fun of his wearing a Speedo and on and on. It touched me because of my own similar experiences I've had over the years.

So I called his swim coach and then I called the baseball coach and explained who I was as well as the situation and, fortunately, I got a coach who was understanding and agreed with me. He agreed that there needed to be that respect. I had the idea of having the guys change sports one day, just for one practice. I said, 'My little swimmer will come to your baseball practice and your baseball player will come to the swimming practice.' And the swimmer loved it: he ran around the track and chased after the balls, while the baseball player, after four laps, stopped, threw up in the gutter and had to get out of the pool. From that moment on, he wrote me letters and talked about how the experience totally changed his life. The swimmer wasn't bullied anymore. And the baseball player stopped picking on him. He even fell in love with the sport.

You don't have to face the world with the weight on your shoulders. My parents understood that, too, but I wanted to show him that there are a lot of people that surround him, who love and care for him. And that goes for everyone: You don't need to face the world yourself. You don't have to feel that way. There are other people around you who love you, whether it's your parents or someone else.

—Rowdy Gaines

Kryptonite and Kellogg's

Rowdy discovered he had a knack for swimming in high school, but he had a long way to go to get from merely good to great. In his world, that meant swimming more — a whole lot more. In fact, he was going to have to double his efforts if he was ever going to get any faster. Easy enough, he thought, only there was one very big hurdle if that was going to actually happen: He needed access to warmer pools.

Practicing with his team in the afternoons was easy for Rowdy. Trying to do that in the mornings, however, was difficult. Cold water was (and still is) one of those absolute impossibilities for him. If he didn't want to be ninety pounds of shivering boy in a Speedo in seventy-degree water, he needed a warm pool to train in.

Easier said than done.

He explains: "I can handle dirty water. I can handle sharks. I can handle waves. I can handle not being able to see. I can handle too much chlorine and I can handle not enough chlorine. I can even handle hot water … but I can't handle cold water, never have."

"It's always been my Kryptonite. I hate it. I've always hated it."

One of the worst cold water experiences he can recall happened in his home state. He was with his friend Lucky Meissenheimer, who has a home on one of the local lakes and conducts something called "Lucky's Lake Swim" on a regular basis. On any given Saturday, between twenty and 250 swimmers gather there to take on the challenge: a 1000-yard swim across the lake and back.

Rowdy had done it many times, but this was different. In this instance, he had a friend in town who wanted to give it a try. Unfortunately, it was in the middle of January. And, contrary to what some may know of Florida, it does get cold in the wintertime. In fact, it was one of the worst winters the state had ever had. The lake temperature was down to fifty degrees.

"When we got there I made up my mind that I was not going to do it. There was no way I was going to swim that lake. Peer pressure is a funny thing, though, even as a fifty-year-old."

Four people were gathered there on that cold, dark morning:

Lucky, his friend Chris, a Special Olympics athlete and Rowdy.

"The three of them talked me into it. I did the swim and I can honestly say I have never been so cold in my life. Even though it only took about fifteen minutes to finish, it took me an hour in Lucky's hot tub to warm back up. I have done the swim many times since but only when the water is eighty degrees or above. I hate cold water."

But his problem was more complicated than that. In small town Winter Haven, there just weren't any public heated pools. They didn't exist. Which was just fine for the summer months, when he could swim to the other side of the lake and back if he felt like it. Once September and October rolled around, he needed a new place to swim.

This is the first (and perhaps only) point in his story where Rowdy had to start breaking the law. He knew of a Quality Inn that had a heated pool and, if he was going to make any progress, it's where he'd have to go – even though he wasn't among the paying guests. And so he did. He walked up, opened the fence, and swam there – day after day, right up until the desk clerk started getting a little suspicious.

"Think about it. There's this one kid, by himself, going to swim at six o'clock in the morning," he says. "I told them the truth and they were sympathetic enough. But because of liability problems, they did what they had to do: They kicked me out."

It wasn't the last time it'd happen. In fact, it was the first in a long line of less-than-favorable exits. And it was the beginning of his spy mission, so to speak, where he was quick to discover other nearby hotels and motels that also had pools he could use, in the mornings, when generally nobody else was using them. He made a running list, scoping out possible scenarios in the afternoons and dropping by to try them out around sunrise.

Some pools were better than others — some were even just the length of a large room — but Rowdy took what he could get, when he could get to it. He'd usually last about a week at a hotel's pool before he'd get found out and he'd have to move on to the next, making his way down the list of six or so, then starting up all over again.

His favorite pool happened to be at a Ramada Inn, but it also required the most precarious planning of them all. If someone were to have caught him in the middle of his daring attempts there and back, they'd have seen a sixteen-year-old boy driving his Volkswagen Beetle a half mile away to the other side of an orange grove (lest they spot it), who'd then run the whole way to a fence he'd jump over, proceeding to swim for an hour, jumping back over the fence when he was finished and, at last, hightailing it back to his car, as fast as he could, half naked and barefoot.

There was a reason for the scantily clad approach.

"It was a long way to go and hard carrying all my stuff over that wall. The less I had on me, the better," he says.

Though he became someone who would trespass out of necessity, he always seemed to bypass any serious trouble as a result. Besides, his mom had always taught him to tell the truth: The less he hid, the better off he'd ultimately be. So he just "put on the blinders" and did what he needed to do.

"I had to do it. Once I had a goal, I knew what I needed to do," he says. "My plan was to earn a scholarship in college. I wanted that. And to get it, I knew I needed to swim fast. Bottom line: Swim fast. That's what I'd do, swimming six days a week, twice a day."

As far as he was concerned, it was necessary. Having been a self-professed late bloomer in his sport, he was having to play catch up. If he was going to surpass those who had been swimming their entire lives, this sort of critical thinking would fast become his norm.

It was during this time that he starting wearing a wetsuit during the chillier months of practice, something that quickly earned him his share of ridicule from the other boys on his team.

It was either that or go back to what he'd been doing. Swim

hard for five minutes, run into a hot shower for the next five, jump back in the pool, on and off again, rinse and repeat, trying hard to keep ahead of the shivers. Too much of that kind of behavior was going to get him kicked off the team.

Not if he beat them to it, that is.

"I almost quit swimming then," Rowdy says, noting the wetsuit his brother-in-law lent him saved him from actually doing so. "I couldn't care less what I looked like because I was a nerd anyway. To be a double nerd didn't much matter to me. They all laughed at me and I was nice and warm. They all wanted wetsuits after that!"

It was after he'd appropriately conquered the cold that the swimming bug really bit. He was closely following the Montreal Olympics in the summer of '76, his first time to really do so. Good choice, too; the 1976 Olympics Men's Swim Team would win twelve of thirteen available gold medals, something that had never happened before or since. They went on to become his role models.

More than three decades later, in 2008, the team won ten of sixteen gold medals; that was the closest they've come to matching what happened the year Rowdy became entranced with the Olympics. The members of the '76 team were the original swimming rock stars. And Rowdy couldn't help but see every last one of them as a hero.

"I wanted to be like them. They were the reasons why I originally wanted to be in the Olympics," he says, confessing his palms still get a little sweaty when he's around any of them today.

And so there was a push from his coaches to not just practice twice a day now, but to practice harder. Whatever it was he was already doing, he had to do it better, faster, bigger than he'd ever done before. He was up to the challenge, too, no matter what it was going to take.

Rowdy didn't live in the pool, not entirely. There were other parts of his life that reflected his strong desire to become an award-winning swimmer, too, a whole side that exposes what some of his trials included on his way towards the top.

Sacrifice became a recurring theme throughout his training. Fast forward to Rowdy's post-college years, some of his leanest. If it meant working as a night clerk in a hotel in order to get to where he wanted to be, he was willing. If it meant not having a proper bed to sleep in and being relegated to sleeping on the floor at day's end — cockroaches crawling across his sleeping bag every single night for a year straight — so be it. And if all he had to survive on were cheap boxes of macaroni and cheese and huge bowls of Cap'n Crunch and Frosted Flakes to give him the energy he so needed, then he'd ask for seconds and thirds and call it good.

He'd made up his mind about that final destination. The journey, on the other hand, was a matter of equal amounts of determination and dedication. Lucky for him, he had both.

"I was going to do anything that was morally and legally right to go to the Olympics. I was going to do anything it took."

His roommate during those years, Dru Dunworth, swam with Rowdy for more than three years in two different schools. He remembers how he and Rowdy lived in what amounted to a dumpy 250 square-foot duplex, an extended-stay joint that would never get mistaken as one of the classiest places in Austin, Texas today.

"Here's a guy who would likely have been the most celebrated swimmer in Olympic history in 1980 and, if he'd lived in Europe, he'd have gone on to be some kind of millionaire," Dru says. "And we were living in what amounted to a kind of crack house."

Not that where he lived much mattered to Rowdy. He would sleep half the day away anyway; all he'd really think about inside of twenty-four hours was whether or not he swam well. It was overhearing people saying he should retire that would get under his skin, Dru says.

"He'd get letters from people claiming he wasn't giving the

teenagers their chance. He was twenty-three years old and considered the old guy! So he was on this constant emotional roller coaster and it was hard to be around him, even kind of depressing."

In addition to the squalor he was living in, Rowdy was driving a white '74 VW Fastback at the time, a car that was so gutless, he'd have to run a stop sign at the bottom of a hill just to make it home after practice. If his gas tank was full, it would weigh his car down so much, he'd just never be able to get it home; he wouldn't be able to make it up that hill.

Barring Sundays, Rowdy's schedule went a little something like this:

6 a.m. to 9 a.m. Swim.
9 a.m. to 2 p.m. Sleep.
3 p.m. to 6 p.m. Swim and train.
7 p.m. to 1 a.m. Work.
1 a.m. to 6 a.m. Sleep.

From the time he'd swum at Auburn on a full athletic scholarship, paying for little more than the car he drove and the gas he'd put in it, to the time his dad showed up on graduation day to haul Rowdy and his belongings down to Austin to train with his old coach, Richard Quick, who had taken on a new coaching position in Texas, he'd gone from living like a king to doing whatever was necessary to survive. He had to pay for everything. And when his waterbed broke en route, he ditched the frame in a baseball field because he just couldn't afford a replacement.

"I didn't have any money and I wasn't about to go back to my parents and ask them for any, especially after they'd helped as much as they had," he says, noting his new so-called bed consisted of whatever he could fashion out of a pile of blankets and a pillow. But, with six hours at the pool each day, he didn't much mind it. He was only there to sleep and eat, anyway. The other hours were spent at his job.

After swimming an average of eight miles a day (or about 480 pool lengths), he worked as a night clerk at a hotel, a position that would have him on his feet for hours. Standing at that point was tougher than it might be normally. But, again, he had a goal. This part of accomplishing it meant working enough over two weeks' time to get a paycheck. Checks were cashed and immediately taken to the grocery store. Whatever wasn't set aside for rent money went to foodstuffs. After all, he had to replace the 8,000-10,000 calories that were being burned every single day.

"Food was so absolutely critical because we were burning fuel like crazy. We were like these big ol' giant Cadillacs … and you need to put gas back into that engine. I could live without electricity, I could even live out on the street, but I had to have food. It was critical to my survival."

As such, a good diet wasn't something he was all too interested in. While he was used to having steaks every other night at Auburn, now he wanted all the carbohydrates he could get his hands on. Big pots of spaghetti with butter to keep it on the cheap. Endless boxes of macaroni and cheese. Just-add-water pancakes.

"Did it get boring? Tiring? Monotonous? Yes, it did! But you did what you had to do," he recalls, noting he knew little to nothing about nutrition at the time. "I still have a hard time looking at those boxes of macaroni and cheese. I tend to get a little nauseous even."

There were no silver platters, no gifted upbringing. Was he competing against swimmers who had private trainers and square meals and plenty of proper rest? He certainly was. But he didn't see them as being any better than he was. He didn't even think he was suffering, not really. It was just what he had to do to get to where he needed to be.

Postscript

In the end, what I did was not that big of a deal. All I did was win a swim race. All the days leading up to it, on the other hand, every single day I was just trying to survive. I loved the feeling of being completely done at day's end because I felt like, if I had put that honest day of work in, I was that much closer to my goal. I was a step closer to where I wanted to be.

You may not be able to imagine actually swimming for ten miles a day, but you certainly can imagine having a goal, working your butt off and wanting to be something or someone in your life, whatever and whoever that actually is. I don't want anyone to think I lived this life of destiny, because that's just not true.

What kept me going was I wanted to be an Olympian. I know that is cliché, but that was my one driving force. I'd always think about being one. Actually competing in an Olympic Games. A real one, one that didn't include a boycott. That was like making it into the Super Bowl, but never being able to play the game.

I knew that, once I reached a certain level, the only thing that would really satisfy me would be to go to the very top. When I went to college, I wanted to win an NCAA championship, I wanted to break a world record and I wanted to win an Olympic gold medal. I never let anybody know those three goals until I had accomplished them. And I did accomplish them — all of them.

—Rowdy Gaines

Critics: Past Prime at 25

As underdog Rowdy Gaines stepped onto the starting block at the 1984 Olympics in Los Angeles, and just seconds from jumping in the pool, he wasn't fixated on missed opportunities from four years earlier.

Yes, he was one of 280 athletes at the top of their game not allowed to compete when Carter decided to boycott the 1980 Games. Yes, Rowdy had made the decision to retire from what he'd done more than all else in his adult life.

Those watching from all over the world knew he had the most at stake being the so-called old guy in the pool at the seasoned age of twenty five years. He was the oldest member of the U.S. men's team. Those he was swimming against were between nineteen and twenty two, holding to their youth and strength and agility as already-won badges of honor.

Three days before the opening ceremonies, the *Chicago Sun-Times* wrote that Rowdy had peaked three years earlier when he swam the 100 Free in 49.36 seconds – faster than anyone in the world. As a twenty-five-year-old, his times for the Olympic trials in Indianapolis were slower than his earlier times and also slower than the times of his nineteen-year-old teammate Mike Heath. In the event Rowdy once ruled – the 200 meter – he didn't even qualify to compete in the Games.

But this time was different than the misfire of 1980. This time he was actually at the Games, in Los Angeles and ready. In his own mind, the odds weren't so stacked against him. Even if some were quick to criticize Rowdy for the attempt, believing he was past his prime and washed up.

Not everyone cast him as the dark horse, though.

Days before the lighting of the symbolic torch, Richard Quick, Rowdy's coach at Auburn and a member of the Olympic staff, said his quarter-century-old protégé was at his peak heading into the 1984 Games.

"Physically, I think Rowdy has the capability to swim faster than he ever has," he said. "He knows he has to swim to win instead of swimming to keep from losing. Any time you're successful over a period of time you have a tendency to defend your position rather than challenging people."

Still, he had a lot to prove, both to others and himself.

In order to fight the voices, the doubts, the naysayers, he sat back in the ready room with a cassette Walkman prior to racing. When he wasn't turning it up as loud as he could to Survivor's "Eye of the Tiger," he was using a cassette with Phil Collins' song "I Don't Care Anymore" on it to block all else out. The louder he turned up the music, the less any of the critics mattered.

Rewind, stop, play. Rewind, stop, play.

Given the circumstances, the song took on all new meaning as it paralleled Rowdy's attempt to gain what was rightfully his four years previous. Collins matched the swimmer's very thoughts with these words:

I don't care what you say
I never did believe you much anyway
I won't be there no more
So get out of my way
Let me by

That small ready room, crammed with some of the world's fiercest competitors, was not a fun place to be. It was intense. Air thick with emotion. Occasional accidental vomiting into nearby trash cans. It was all Rowdy could do to try and block out where he was and look toward where he would be and what he would be doing.

In the 1982 World Championships, he hadn't been so lucky. An athlete from East Germany showed up an hour before their race together and decided he was going to be the swimmer's shadow; he followed him around the entire time. Even in the bathroom, the athlete hovered behind him. Neither spoke the other's language but, then again, neither necessarily needed to.

The previous three years, Rowdy and this same swimmer – Jorge Woithe – had gone back and forth in the world rankings. Still, neither had raced against the other. The only thing Rowdy knew about him was his name.

It wasn't until right before his race he realized the person who had followed him around wasn't necessarily Jorge. The East German team had assigned someone else to stick close to Rowdy and get in his head while Jorge had been in the back resting. But it didn't much matter at that point. The damage had been done.

"He beat me," Rowdy says. "He beat me by three one-hundredths of a second."

Whether those swimming against him in this new arena viewed it as such or not, Rowdy had something the others lacked: Good, old-fashioned experience. It was on his side; it was in his corner. Imagine training in various pools four years straight, swimming ten-plus miles of laps a day, six days a week, fifty-two weeks out of the year, taking a few days of a break and then doing it all over again. That was his routine, his reality even. He simply had no choice but to move forward.

If he wanted to have a shot at calling himself an Olympian, this was it. If he missed out on it this time, the danger was that it could have been his last shot. It was something his dad had warned him about; if he was going to live a long life, taking four extra years out of it in order to achieve a lifelong dream was simply putting a few drops in a big bucket.

It was that pep talk that would eventually lead to Los Angeles.

"All of a sudden, my four-year journey became an eight-year journey," Rowdy remembers. And that journey of eight years was actually even a lot longer than that.

"While it's assumed I started later than most," he says, "I felt like the day I started swimming in a wetsuit in high school in freezing cold water was when my training for the Olympics really began."

There was plenty at stake, too, especially if he were to fully accomplish his goals. It wasn't enough to have broken a long list of world records or to have received accolade after accolade while he was at Auburn. This was way beyond placing first in his state championships in high school. It was his shot at being the best in the world at one of the oldest documented sports on the planet.

This was the big time, his big time. Rowdy was prepared to reclaim his lost hopes of 1980. As that was the case, he had to prove his worth. He believed in himself and all he could do; he didn't want to let those who believed in him down, either.

"In swimming, we didn't have a World Series or Super Bowl to aspire to, still don't," Rowdy says. "Our highest level was the Olympics. It's all we had. It's all we cared about. And it's every four years, not every year."

And so he took a deep breath and walked out to the pool. This wasn't the Floridian stomping ground of his youth and this certainly wasn't Moscow in 1980. This was Los Angeles. There were 25,000 people cheering for the swimmers there, but they weren't cheering for just any of them … they yelled as loudly as they could for the barefoot Americans. Those were the ones Rowdy could hear.

"Once I got to the deck, I could feel the energy. It was undeniable. I could just feel the crowd from where I stood."

And, in his head, Rowdy was thinking about how he'd paid his dues to get to this point. He looked around at those he was about to compete against and he knew, he absolutely knew, they hadn't been through all he had. After all, he was the only one there who'd qualified for the team in 1980. This didn't mean he would win against the lot of them. To him, it just meant that he should. That's what made the most sense.

He looked around at these others who hadn't been where he'd been and he felt like he'd done more, seen more, sacrificed more than every one of them. Still, he couldn't shake the notion that it might be okay for him to come in second or third or even fourth place.

It was a shield of sorts, a protection from being even more nervous than he was already.

"I'd think, 'I'm an Olympian. I'm in the Games. I've had a great career. It doesn't matter how I swim.' But deep down I was afraid, of one thing and only one: I was afraid of not winning."

Rowdy will joke that, up to this point, he had just three people to impress on the sidelines — his mom, his dad and his coach —

and that was as many people as had ever seen him race anywhere, in the countless number of races he'd tackled. Because there were filled bleachers and cameras rolling and an entire world watching from their couches and television sets, the pressure was on. The stakes were considerably higher.

It happened fast. But, before he knew it, he was jumping toward the pool. He'd started his race. And, for the most part, everything was a blur. A very, very fast blur. Only there was one thing on his mind, at least initially: He'd had to change his start based on a tip his coach had given him.

"And the start and the turn are the two most critical components of the 100 Free. On my start, I was notorious for coming down slow on the command, so I could keep my motion going.

"I swam on the third day of the Olympics. Normally, there are two or three starters at an Olympic Games and they rotate. You never know which starter you're going to get. They all have their own style to start a race. You can't necessarily study a starter because of the way they rotate. However, on the first day, there was a starter who was very quick on his command and the time he shot the gun to start the race. My coach saw that guy start a race and he came to me and told me we had to change my start. If you don't come down and get set quickly, there's a chance you'll be left on the blocks."

It wasn't the most well-received news.

"I was freaking out! For two years, I'd been doing the exact same start and I didn't want to change it!" he says. "But that's where my trust came in and I said, 'Okay, let's do it.'"

"And my coach told me I might get someone slow, but I might get this guy too. In the finals, at the beginning of my race, there he was. If my coach had not come to me and done what he did and said what he said, there's a good chance I would have lost."

One thing he did know is he was prepared. He was so ready to swim that specific race, he could do so with his eyes closed. And he very regularly did just that. When he wasn't able to be in the pool, he'd lie in bed at night, stopwatch in hand, and swim the race in his head, over and over again. When he'd finished, he would hit the stopwatch, open his eyes, and be within two or three tenths of a second of 49.3, the exact time he wanted to break.

As for trying to piece together any other thoughts during that brief race? They're a little harder to grasp.

"I remember flipping at the wall and flipping first and thinking I'm in the lead and I'm not hurting. And I usually am at the fifty. It's hard to remember anything about how I was feeling.

Everything is race, strategy. You're thinking about the next step. I'm not thinking, 'If I win this I can't wait to see my mom and dad.' There's no time to do anything else. You're wrapped up in what you're trying to accomplish."

When it was over, though, that's another story entirely. Once he completed his race, he didn't immediately know who had won, but that didn't matter to him at first. Rowdy was savoring these moments, stretching them into long minutes, not wanting any of it to end.

"I remember touching and hearing the crowd erupt," he says. "But, I'm thinking to myself, there are two Americans in the race. My first thought is, well, I have a fifty-fifty chance of having won – it was either me or the other guy. Since our room had overlooked the pool ever since the Games had started, I knew what that crowd sounded like when an American won a race. It had to have been one of us."

And so, Rowdy waited. He waited for the inevitable. If he'd lost, he had these seconds to pretend otherwise; he would at least feel for a time as if he'd come out the victor. On the other hand, if he'd won, it would be a different kind of scene altogether. He did turn around, but he was in no rush to do so.

"I wanted to relish the cheer from the crowd and think for at least a moment that it was me who'd won … even if it was for a split second. And, when I looked at the board, I didn't even look for my time — you just don't look for times. I looked and saw a No. 1 by my name and it was like a balloon popped and all the pressure wilted away and I started going nuts."

"It's a joy that is hard to describe. The pinnacle. Knowing I was hanging on by a thin thread for dear life at the end and I knew it, to have it all culminate in that one race, it's beyond description."

For Rowdy, once he'd finished a race, he was usually exhausted, just spent. He wouldn't even be able to get out of the pool right away. This time around, he was so filled with adrenaline, he wasn't even breathing very hard. If the powers that be had asked him to do another 100 just for kicks, he'd have easily been able to do so, and gladly. He almost wanted to even.

Attach any single word to how Rowdy was feeling — ecstatic, relieved, baffled, take your pick — but it's hard to say any of them completely matched up with his grab bag of emotions.

"With the exception of my children being born, that was the single-most thrilling moment I've ever had in my life," he says. "It was just this feeling of pure and total joy welling up inside me."

That joy led to him raising his fist triumphantly in the air and beaming. While he hadn't planned for how he would react, those watching poolside were ready to do so along with him. Which is to say they lost it, just as he did.

"The adrenaline was so strong at that point … you get so excited about something that you remember the feeling you have, but you're unaware of your surroundings. For me, World War III could have been happening. Naked women could have been prancing around and I wouldn't have noticed. I remember nothing else happening."

When American Rick Carey had won shortly before him, snagging a gold medal for the United States for the 200 Backstroke, Rick wasn't all that happy with himself. He'd wanted to break the world record during his race and, when that failed to happen, he hit the wall in disgust after winning. And, when the National Anthem played later, he stood, almost dejectedly, with his head down the entire time.

Rowdy remembers an audience that turned on his teammate, some even throwing out scattered boos when Carey was on the podium.

"The thing is, the Olympics has nothing to do with time, even though that's usually the first thing you look at as a swimmer," he explains. "Usually it's all about getting your personal best time, but the Olympics is the one race it just doesn't matter. Rick's goal was beating his best time and, when that didn't happen, it was as if he had lost the race, at least in his mind.

"Times are thrown out the window. They're irrelevant. Everything is about placing, how you place. If you get eighth, you're in the Top Eight. If you get ninth, you don't get into the finals. If you're fourth, you miss a medal. If you're silver, you miss the gold."

Rowdy hadn't broken a world record with his time, one he had already held. He had, however, gone faster than any other swimmer in the 100.

"When I heard the crowd going crazy when I started to go nuts, I think they were thinking to themselves: 'Here's a guy who knows how to celebrate.' They just got higher and higher when I started throwing up my fist. They were ready."

As was he.

As the cheers escalated, he remained in the pool, taking it all in. The past eight years of his life had been worth all the sacrifice and heartache it had taken to get here.

"You know how you talk to God sometimes? I said, 'If you let me feel this way again, I'll go through eight more years of training and setbacks all over again for this split second of a feeling.'

"I think if I'd have raced ten more times, I'd probably have been beat nine of them. But that was my one race of perfection … the most perfect race I've ever swum in my life."

The French call this *La Volupte*, this feeling of discovering a sense of rhythm that doesn't include pain or suffering, the ability to reach beyond and seize perfection. Rowdy found it that day.

When he did get out of the pool, when he knew he couldn't drag it out any further, the first person he laid eyes on was his coach, Richard Quick, the man who'd seen his journey from almost the very beginning. The two men embraced each other and couldn't help but burst out in tears.

Next, he immediately looked for his family. He had no idea where they were sitting. He looked toward the cheering crowd and hoped to pick out his mom, dad and sister. He looked and he looked, but he couldn't find a single one of them.

"My parents were a huge part of who I was then and who I am now," he explains. "It meant so much to me that they were there."

When he finally found them a short while later, they'd been moved from what they referred to as their nosebleed seats to somewhere near the front, so they could see their son and brother accept his first gold medal. Someone in security had located his mom and sister and allowed them that rare opportunity.

After winning the gold, singing the National Anthem.

That moment is captured in a photograph Rowdy's dad Buddy has hanging in his bedroom at Little Gasparilla Island. He shines a flashlight on it when it's too dark to see it and quickly lets on that it's one of his very favorite photos, one he's afforded the title, aptly enough, "Sheer Joy." Even showing it off more than thirty years after it happened allows him to tap into the past and stir up some emotions.

As much as time has allowed life to progress in a thousand unique directions, some just tend to stay the same. Case in point: When Rowdy's dad is close to tears, he makes no attempt to hide them.

"My parents were opposites," Rowdy says. "I would say to my dad something like, 'Hey! I just broke a world record!' and he'd say 'That's nice. What did you do in school today?' My mom, on the other hand, would absolutely be cheering: 'Oh, Lord, hallelujah!'"

At the Olympics, however, the tables quickly turned when he nabbed one win, and then another and then another, three gold medals in all. He came to the Olympics as a newly minted Olympian and was able to leave as three-time gold medal winner Rowdy Gaines. He was not just the oldest member of his Olympic team, but, at that point in history, he was one of the oldest in the sport to win gold.

"When I walked out after winning, it was this total opposite reaction from my parents. My mom gave me a quick hug and, when I saw my dad, he just fell to his knees. My dad was an emotional guy but had always played it cool with me and my swimming. Now, all of a sudden, he was balling like a baby.

"And to see those barriers break down and know he had it all inside for a long time and was able to release it was a huge joy. My mom wore her emotions on the outside so much, she had nothing left to give. She was done."

As for why he won, he might have a different reason for every person who has ever asked him the question. In fact, depending on who's doing the asking, he might say that there were others who should have come out ahead of him, but didn't.

"I should have been fifth. There were four guys who should have beaten me in '84, at least physically. Mentally is where I won the race. I believed I deserved to win. And not in the sense that I was a better person than they were, but I know there's no way they could have worked harder than I had."

That one perfect race was preceded by a night without sleep, a good two-hour nap to combat it, a warm-up in the pool, a picture-perfect weather day and relatively little smog. With all the pieces having fallen together as they did, it's of little wonder he was calm and collected when it came time to perform. All strategic things considered, he'd swum a perfect race.

"There are so many little things to consider that fell into place. I was scared to death, but a calm had come over me. I'd been a basket case for two years straight and couldn't relax, but this was something entirely different.

"I watch the Olympics sometimes and I think 'Wouldn't it be cool to do that?' And my wife says, 'You're crazy! You did do that!' That's the half of me that doesn't recognize the person or the achievement. The other half of me remembers. I remember my coach hugging me and walking out to the national anthem."

His gold medals would soon go to the three people who helped him win them — his dad, his mom, his coach — but that didn't necessarily take away or detract from the champion he had become and the races he'd won. Rowdy had done what he had set out to do.

"This eight-year journey culminated in a race that lasted forty-nine seconds. We had our last relay and were sitting around talking about how many miles we had swum to get to this point and we discovered I had swum over 20,000 miles all inclusive. And, to be completely honest, I wouldn't change one mile or take one mile away. It defined me as a person. I joke that the rest of my life is going to be a piece of cake, because nothing would be harder than what I'd gone through to win. And so winning, in effect, taught me a lot of lessons. It taught me dedication, commitment, teamwork, setting goals. And, to this day, I still have that. I have all of that."

Rowdy and World Record relay teammates — the only relay in history in which all four were individual world record holders

Postscript

Never give up. Never give up on your dreams. We dream about stuff. We dream about being a good writer or a great doctor. My dream was to win an Olympic gold medal. Winning taught me that I was happy I didn't give up, even though I wanted to, thought about it and even did along the way.

Winning was proof that hard work does pay off. It makes me tired thinking of all the miles I swam, but every single stroke was worth it. The value of that was well worth it. Having said that, the value of that dedication would have been there even if I hadn't won. It taught me an honest day's work and what it could lead to later in life.

I was never great academically. Today I think I can be a better father and husband and son. I think I can be a better worker and businessman, whatever it is. I can be better at my job. I don't necessarily feel like a winner, but I'm not a loser, either. I feel like I'm trying to do the best I can in all of those areas. Nobody can ask you to do more than your best.

I'm trying to do the best I can with what I feel. We're capable of doing better. I'm proud of the kind of person I am. I don't steal, cheat or lie. I'm faithful. I think I'm going to go to heaven. I feel like I've been a pretty good person. I think God's going to look at me and say I'm a winner. I've done pretty good in my life. And, if it ends tomorrow, I can look back and say, that's what I want people to remember me by.

—Rowdy Gaines

Parades, Pitfalls and a Path

"Some people might think it's an unfortunate thing, but my life was defined with that race in the Olympics. On my gravestone, the epitaph will probably read 'Olympic Gold Medalist,' and I'm okay with that. I'm proud of that."

When Rowdy walked away from the Olympics a decorated swimmer, three new gold medals in tow, he'd accomplished something so incredible, so unbelievably challenging, it served to define the rest of his life. He joined a small, elite group of athletes who made history winning at that level. While he didn't immediately know all that lay in store for his future — it was like diving headfirst into a whirlwind — it did come with a ready swimming theme attached. And this before any Olympic swimmer had ever built a career as a direct result of their successes. Lucky for him, he knew a thing or two about that world.

For a man who once believed graduating from college meant leaving swimming behind for an entirely new career, he broke with tradition by doing things altogether differently than most: He allowed his passion for the sport to define all he did and he wrote his own playbook along the way.

Initially, though, there was a time when he assumed he'd become a movie director and follow in his dad's footsteps. A huge fan of the movies, Rowdy had studied filmmaking in college and he knew he could lean on his dad if he ever needed the support. There was even a half-formed plan to work with Buddy in Chicago after the Olympics, only that never quite happened.

"The Olympics changed the direction of my life," Rowdy says. "Winning took me on a different journey."

He's quick to liken the opportunities that followed the Olympics to coming out on top at the television show American Idol. Its competitors have largely sung for years on end. And actually winning the competition and earning the inevitable exposure that follows? That's what allows them to soar far beyond their greatest original intentions.

And so it was for Rowdy. He swam for a live televised audience of what amounted to over two billion fans the world over.

Just like that, he moved from being a relative unknown to being recognized everywhere he went.

His mom can back that up. Speaking with Jettie from the front room of her home, photographs and posters of her son covering most hallways and wall space like some one-of-a-kind wallpaper, she recalls things in fairly vivid detail. She was at the Olympic Village just after Rowdy won, after all, when the crowds were grabbing hold of the newly minted swimmer, pulling on his shirt and stepping on her to get to him.

"And I thought, my God, he's a celebrity."

Once he returned home to Winter Haven, that sort of scene more or less repeated itself. A big parade was put on at Cypress Gardens in Rowdy's honor. The whole town put things on hold to come out and meet their hero.

"People were acting like he was a rock idol, even pulling buttons off his jacket," Jettie says with a fair amount of incredulity. "I've never seen anything like that before. I thought … this is my son!"

If the parade wasn't enough, there was that full page ad in the local newspaper, the Winter Haven News Chief. It had all the signs from the local businesses photographed, each offering their own "Welcome back!" to the decorated swimmer. There were the thousands of people who'd gathered, filling the streets and eager to catch their own personal glimpses of the Olympian. There was a six-foot-tall cake and the mayor on hand to help present it. There were aunts and uncles and grandparents and more.

All in all, it amounted to total pandemonium. That fact was not lost on young Rowdy.

"It's safe to say my life changed pretty dramatically, even though I'd been doing this for eight years," he recalls. Bleacher seats began filling up more than they once had. He went from that skinny blonde guy who swam all the time to someone who had his own growing fan club, some kind of a following even.

As much as they showered him with praise, Rowdy's celebrity extended far beyond Winter Haven. He was being invited as a guest of The Tonight Show. He traveled to Washington, D.C. to meet the president of the United States. Disney World even shut down so he and the other Olympic champions could enjoy the rides without waiting in a single line.

"I couldn't have dreamt this stuff up," he admits. "It was pretty spectacular."

At the time Rowdy competed, Los Angeles was considered the epicenter of all things media-related. The 1984 Olympics became what would be known thereafter as the "media" Olympics. Thanks to organizer Peter Ueberroth, it revolved around sponsorship too. It's all too common in sports now, but it had never before happened with the Games. Even the pool Rowdy swam in was sponsored by a corporation — a little mom and pop fast food chain known as McDonald's.

Sponsorship suddenly became a way of subsidizing the enormous expense that is the Olympics without jeopardizing the cities so intent on hosting them. In fact, the '84 Games made a healthy profit of over $200 million, the first time for the Games to make money since 1932 (The Independent, "After The Party: What happens when the Olympics leaves town," 8/8/2008). Coincidentally, those Games also took place in Los Angeles.

Normally, the Olympics would lose money, not earn it. For example, according to the Canadian Press, it took Montreal more than three decades to pay off the bills it encountered hosting the 1976 Olympic Games.

A short history lesson: Before the 1984 Games, the Olympics were more or less nonexistent for the United States for eight years (the result of the 1980 boycott). The Games in 1972 were marred by the tragic events and deaths in Munich when eleven Israeli athletes and coaches and a West German police officer were killed. And, in Mexico

City in 1968, the usual celebrations were overshadowed by two African-American athletes (Tommie Smith and John Carlos) each raising an arm in a Black Power salute while on the podium. It's widely regarded as one of the most overtly political statements in the history of the Olympics.

Having an Olympics happen in the United States after having gone so long without one was as much a celebration as it was a huge step forward. And the Los Angeles Games became a way of trading financial suffering for professionalism. Those in charge allowed athletes to both compete and make money doing so when they had never been allowed that opportunity.

At long last, athletes were given the green light to earn money while devoting themselves to their sports.

"I felt like we were the Rod Lavers and Stan Smiths of the day," Rowdy says.

He identifies with Laver and Smith because of how similar their plight once was to that of the Olympic swimmer. While none of them held accolades in the pool, they were exceptional at what it was they did, having once dominated the tennis court. Laver holds over 200 career titles. Smith won major titles all over the world. Tennis used to be an amateur sport: None of its star players were allowed to earn on their winnings, no matter how good they were. So it was with swimming: There was no such thing as being a pro swimmer.

Not until the '84 Games, that is.

"The powers that be couldn't stop it from happening anymore," Rowdy says. "Too many other countries were paying their athletes."

How did it affect Rowdy personally? In 1983, he earned a grand total of $1,200. In 1984, he made $150,000 ... and that was all in the last six months of the year.

Financial boost aside, Rowdy hadn't prepared for his next step. He'd set out to achieve a goal — a colossal one at that — and now he was in uncharted territory. What now? What was he supposed to do? He didn't have a lot of ideas.

"I wanted to jump off a building," he says.

Post competition depression is a real, even common, condition especially for Olympic athletes, and Rowdy found himself in the thick of it. Training and practice and entire lifestyle adjustments had dominated his life for years. And whether Olympians win or lose, there's a real danger they'll lose their sense of purpose once the competitions are over.

In Rowdy's case, the one thing that defined him for so long was done. It was over with. He couldn't help but be overwhelmed by a sense of loss.

"I really didn't know what to expect," he says. "I didn't know that the day after I finished it was going to be a whole new life for me. I thought, what in the world am I going to do with my life now? I had this feeling of … is this the only thing I know how to do … swim?"

He was able to work through it, but depression came back to haunt him just five years later, in 1988. It was a great personal year for Rowdy but he's quick to call it the most depressing year of his life professionally. It's not hard to see why. At a loss for what to do, he'd pursued and received his real estate license; he was selling condos on a golf course in Palm Beach. Only he wasn't exactly selling them. It was not uncommon for him to be in an office from nine to five and not have a single customer for five days straight. He whiled away the hours playing Contra or Pac Man on the Nintendo, so much that he ended up suffering from tennis elbow.

Any extracurricular activities related to swimming had dried right up.

"I didn't do anything that year – no traveling, no speeches, no clinics. And that scared me to death."

It was 1988, which meant all-new Olympians had come along, a whole fresh crop of talent. Rowdy had been able to ride the wave of stardom between 1984 and 1988, but new names and stars had suddenly taken precedence.

Luckily, it wasn't exactly final. Things did pick up. He started to earn income from his name and knowledge alone. That's when he had an idea.

"I thought maybe I could build a name for myself and be the person people came to if they wanted an expert on swimming."

It worked. It's still working to this day; he's been a real presence in the sport in every capacity imaginable. Consider the following: He's a broadcaster, a swim coach, a clinician, a public speaker, an active competitor and part of many, many charitable events too.

Rowdy is like the Swiss Army knife of the swimming world, able to tackle most directions and do most things. This has allowed him to become an invaluable resource, a gift that continually gives.

"When somebody says, 'Let's get a swimmer,' my name tends to pop up," he says. "You name it, there's no area of swimming I haven't touched."

Digging a little deeper, there are a couple of large reasons he has succeeded at making swimming his career, at least in his eyes. One has to do with the boycott. He forged through a very difficult time and that resonated with broad audiences. Being widely regarded as the best in his sport in 1980, then having the opportunity to compete taken away, then still managing to return and win, well, everybody likes a comeback story. What's more, they like to hear it told.

Second, having the Olympics on the shores of his own country after eight years worked to Rowdy's advantage. He won when people – namely, Americans – were starving for an Olympics. It's a good reason Mary Lou Retton became a household name; she quickly resonated with the United States of America as the country's sweetheart. Here was a whole nation looking for something and Rowdy helped give the people what it was they wanted to see.

"That's a combination I was able to build on," he says. "There has to be a reason you want to pull for someone and, lucky for me, I was the benefactor of that. I'd waited eight years to do what I did."

And from a Madison Avenue standpoint, he says, that's the kind of perseverance that matters.

Working closely with the Olympics as a spokesperson and speaker between 1984 and 1988 put Rowdy in a good position, but the tides started shifting after that point. In the year that followed, he was earning less than half of what he'd typically made annually the previous four years. He went from talking to his agent on a daily basis to maybe talking with him monthly. But he didn't let that get him down. Quite the contrary. It was an experience that served to motivate him.

What if he could build a brand that stretched beyond swimming? Who wouldn't relate to a personal story of overcoming significant obstacles? So he rebranded and redesigned his own experiences to make them even more relatable to others, making his story less of a sports story and more universal in tone.

The worry and fear is, of course, what happens if and when all of this ekes towards a natural stop? At what point in time will the endorsements, broadcast opportunities and speaking invitations begin to fade out or, worse yet, disappear?

Ask that question and it plays right into fears that have never fully gone away. In fact, he has mentioned that things already feel like they're starting to go that way, that this next Olympics in Rio may be his last go-round. His wife will say it's something he's alluded to happening for the last three Olympic Games. But, every single time, all the television stations and networks ask him back again and renew his contracts, almost like clockwork.

"Still, who knows what will happen after Rio? I'm beginning to see the light at the end of the tunnel," Rowdy says. "In 2020, I'll be sixty-one years old. There's a solid chance that, not too many years from now, I'll be done with everything."

"I try to look at the people who've come before me, those who I've looked up to," Rowdy says, speaking about sports commentators who've also played similar roles. John Madden and Dick Button were two commentators he emulated for years on end, and they each lasted into their sixties and seventies before retiring.

As far as he was concerned, Madden and Button knew what they were talking about and he always respected them for it. And for his part, he only wants to broadcast as long as he can stay relevant at what he's doing and so long as he knows what he's talking about, too. He wants others to feel the same way toward him. Luckily, he still feels like he's friends with the swimmers he's granted the opportunity to speak with. He doesn't feel like they look at him and ask why their grandfather is on deck. As long as he can keep up with new terminology as it evolves, as long as his conversations still make a fair amount of sense and as long as he understands where it is "these kids" are coming from, he's going to keep at it. Besides, he likes what he's doing.

To see his schedule is to marvel at the breakneck pace he lives every day. He dedicates himself to speaking to audiences of students, business leaders and boys and girls clubs. He leads clinics and competitions for Masters swimmers, which is a group of more than 60,000 competitive swimmers from age eighteen to more than ninety. He also serves as a part-time spokesman and supporter of The Limu Company, a growing marketing company in central Florida. It's just one of nearly a dozen sponsors he still enjoys. In addition, he's vice president of Aquatics at the Central Florida YMCA in Orlando, where he clocks in each weekday. And he's never stopped broadcasting for a number of television networks and colleges throughout the country.

When he announces for the 2016 Olympics in Brazil, it'll be his seventh time doing so. That will make him the very longest-running Olympic commentator for the sport he is so devoted to.

He's quick to say that he's busier now than he's ever been. A lot of that has to do with swimming being on television a whole lot more than it was fifteen years ago. He'll be flying back and forth and broadcasting on location for more than fifteen events this year alone, five times the average amount he used to do. Why do they keep asking him back? Much of that has to do with, he says, the reputation he's built for himself over time.

"People trust I'll have integrity when I represent them," he says, adding it's taken him thirty years to arrive at this point. "I think they know what they're getting when they hire me."

Would winding things down be something his family might like a lot? Probably. If nothing else, it would allow him to know where he's going to swim from one day to the next. And it's not that he's counting the days to retirement or anything, but consider that he had his first commentating gig in 1986. He knows better than anyone else that he's had a good run.

"I didn't get to watch my kids grow up too much," he says. "So when that time comes to pass my mic on to the next guy, I think I'll be ready."

In his still far-off future, he sees himself spending a considerable amount of time at a beach house on the small island where his dad and stepmother now reside where, in his own words, he'll do "absolutely nothing."

Until then, he'll get to continue meeting some of the best swimmers in the world. He'll get to be on hand to talk about them and see all the instant replays. He'll get to continue being around the sport he loves so much. He'll also continue to speak to others about being water safe. To that point, he mentions a mother and father who lost their child to drowning. Now they're dedicated to helping educate others on pool safety, doing all they can to ensure a similar scenario isn't repeated.

"I have tremendous admiration and respect for that mother and father," Rowdy says of the parents Brian and Karen Cohn, who have created the ZAC Foundation in memory of their son. "I get to help them share their vision."

Postscript

I've said this before but I didn't swim to be popular. I swam because I loved it. And the Olympics changed that. And it gets popular every four years. It's brief, but for about two weeks, swimming is the most popular sport in the land. People know all about it. The wins were for my sport, not so much for me. I knew my fame would be fleeting, but I was proud my sport was put on the map.

I owe swimming more than it's ever owed me. I was able to represent USA Swimming for eight years and they still feel like family.

Even now, I feel like I'm the luckiest guy in the world. I'm very fortunate. Not many Olympians can say that. I work for a great organization, YMCA, and I have a swimsuit sponsor and I just signed a deal with Liberty Mutual. Do I see my life changing in ten years? After thirty-plus years, I'm still doing okay. And after another thirty, I'll be alright too.

You can't tell someone, 'Well, I was a swimmer and I did pretty good.' Because they're going to always follow it with two questions. The first is 'Did you go to the Olympics?' and the second is 'Did you win a gold medal?' Like it or not, it's how many swimmers are defined in the media.

—Rowdy Gaines

Paralyzed

Guillain-Barre Syndrome is a disorder that can occasionally be fatal and occurs when the body's defense (immune) system mistakenly attacks part of the nervous system. This leads to nerve inflammation that causes muscle weakness and more. In short, it's paralysis — even of respiratory systems.

There's an uncommonly dark period in Rowdy's life that gets glossed over and pushed aside. It's too painful for all involved to want to say much about it. Some would rather forget it even happened. Others go so far as to call it the very worst time in their lives. Rowdy doesn't talk much about the disease that struck him suddenly in 1991, when he was thirty-two years old, running a sports club in Honolulu and training to possibly qualify for the Barcelona Olympics the following year.

The crux of it is this: There was a time when Rowdy became so unbelievably and surprisingly sick, he might have never swum another stroke or even survived. He mysteriously contracted Guillain-Barre Syndrome, a disease that strikes about one in 100,000 victims annually. It left him completely paralyzed from his neck down for three months. It meant he couldn't articulate simple words very well, ate his meals through feeding tubes and lost fifty pounds – dropping from 170 to 120 – in a few months. It's the closest Rowdy has ever come to dying.

It's understandable that no one who watched Rowdy endure the debilitating disease wants to revisit that period, especially his immediate family members. The experience, though, helped him solidify and strengthen his then still-new relationship of four years with his wife, Judy, and two small girls.

Rowdy's mother doesn't mince words when she describes her feelings about what happened.

"That was the very worst thing to happen in my life, that week he went into the hospital," Jettie recalls, fighting tears. She admits Hawaii doesn't hold many good memories for her, even decades later.

No one can say with certainty how he contracted it. But once he did, the first tendrils of the disease took hold quickly.

In the summer of 1991, Rowdy and Judy traveled to Connecticut for a Swim Across America event. Participants swam and raced across the Long Island Sound raising money for cancer research. It was business as usual; they had been involved with the organization for some time (and continue to be). Only this time fast became markedly different from the others. It was here Rowdy started not feeling quite right. In fact, upon returning to his hotel room after the event, everything started moving in slow motion for him and he felt loopy. It was almost like he'd had too much to drink and he had a pins-and-needles sensation in his fingers and toes.

While he didn't exactly know what to make of it, he quickly diagnosed himself as having the flu. When he visited his family doctor the same day he returned to Hawaii, the doctor was on board with Rowdy's diagnosis. Why yes, it certainly was the flu, he said, nothing more. That was that.

The pins-and-needles sensation would spread from Rowdy's hands and feet to his arms and legs. He wasn't even able to feel his hands when he'd clench them together. On top of that, going up and down the steps at his home was becoming increasingly difficult for the young athlete … and there were only four steps to tackle. Still, Rowdy wanted to shake it off. He resisted all suggestions he go to the hospital for an expert opinion, even though whatever it was he was feeling wasn't going away. Besides, he was at the top of his game physically and felt it would pass soon enough. Up to that point in his life, he'd gone to the hospital just once and it was an overnight stay to get his tonsils out. How bad could this really be?

One day as he was heading up the stairs to the Oahu Club, which he managed, his breathing became difficult. Judy was at his side and later recalled him saying he couldn't even walk up into the club.

At that point, she insisted he go immediately to the hospital.

When Judy insisted he get checked out once again and he finally cooperated, about twenty-four hours after he'd first started to feel bad, he had to lean on her all the way out to their car. Whatever it was had progressed. He could feel his strength waning.

"Once we got to the hospital, she was lucky enough to get a doctor in town who knew what it was I had," Rowdy recalls. "And he said that if I hadn't have come in when I did, I could have died."

When someone contracts Guillain-Barre Syndrome (what their new doctor fast determined Rowdy had), his or her nervous system slowly shuts down, bit by bit, until it ceases to function altogether. And, as that is exactly what a person depends on to control their breathing, the results can be ultimately fatal without immediate medical attention. About 5 percent of those who contract the condition never recover.

Rowdy didn't know he faced a potentially life threatening disease, at least not yet. Once admitted to the hospital, he didn't feel as healthy as he could have at that point. But he just wanted the quick fix that would help him mend. He was after whatever medicine or antibiotic he needed to get so he could clear things up and be on his way. He had a life to lead, a family to care for, more time to spend in the pool, a gym to run … and that list went on.

At least that's where his head was when a neurologist came in and completely changed his thinking. He told Rowdy that, unless something was done immediately, he would need to be placed on the iron lung. And, when his patient didn't appear to know what that meant entirely, the doctor explained further.

"He said, 'Your breathing is shutting down … you are losing the ability to breathe on your own.' And that's when I started getting worried," Rowdy said.

He had every reason to be. Within twenty-four hours of being admitted to the hospital in Honolulu, three-time Olympic gold medalist Rowdy Gaines was completely paralyzed from the neck down. No one could have expected it would get as bad as it did, as fast as it did.

"Of course we thought he'd just be in the hospital short term," Judy recalls. "He was in such good shape, so we naturally didn't assume the worst."

And, according to her, she couldn't consider that he might not come home altogether. She simply couldn't. With each passing hour, Rowdy's body became weaker and discussion turned to respiratory failure. What they thought would be a short few days of a visit turned into weeks upon weeks of plasmapheresis treatments. To begin that process, they installed a port in his chest underneath his left clavicle to remove his blood. A large machine spun the liquid at a high revolution to separate the viral plasma. It then pumped into him a human blood product rich with the protein powers of albumin.

That new, painful process of washing the blood and returning it to the body would cause Rowdy to automatically scream out in pain whenever it took place. Judy recalled how difficult it was to listen to him scream and cry out.

"We just held his hands and we both just waited for it to be over," she said.

In addition to that pain, he felt tremendous nausea, had stomach cramps and was bitterly cold, to the point he could almost never stop shivering — even with multiple electric blankets heaped on top of him.

It was something Judy wasn't accustomed to hearing or seeing, but she was determined to be the strong one for him and the rest of their family. Judy's mother, Connie Zachea, played a critical role by caring for young Emily and Madison during the vigil. Judy was at the hospital, trading shifts with Jettie, tending to a six- and two-year-old at home when she wasn't at his side. And, while it was difficult and she admits to shedding her share of tears when she was far away from Rowdy's bedside, "you kind of go into survival mode."

"They thought he might have even had lymphoma and maybe cancer on top of everything else. So, yes, I had my fears," she recalls. "But you can't walk into the room of a person you love and let them see that."

She knew that, if she did, it would affect his recovery time. She was determined to be his strength when he didn't have much strength to call his own. She took on the fears he was feeling.

It helped that Rowdy was in peak physical condition when he contracted the disease. It helped that he was in the hospital amongst experienced medical practitioners. Also, he had the will to want to get better, though that took some time to develop. When the iron lung was wheeled into his room and they began to make preparations to connect him to it, one of the technicians bent down and whispered in his ear. Rowdy recalls him saying, "Believe me, you do not want to be on this thing. If you're on it, you could end up in here even longer … you could be here six months. You could get pneumonia. You could even die from being on that thing."

Taking in the monstrosity that was the iron long, Rowdy believed the technician right away. For the unfamiliar, an iron lung is a rigid metal case that's fitted over a patient's body and it's used for administering prolonged artificial respiration by means of mechanical pumps. That's the textbook definition. Imagine a long heavy metal case that a person's full body goes inside and only his head pokes out. One might easily assume, given the choice, nobody would actually want to be inside of one.

There wasn't a lot he remembers from that time of his life. He remembers not being able to pick up his daughter Madison and her crying as a result. He recalls good friend Dick Carson visiting and a massage therapist who came in to help with his pain now and again. But that technician talking with him is still crystal clear in his mind.

"He was telling me I needed to start fighting or I could be in big trouble. It scared me straight. It was like going to jail," Rowdy says. "My breathing was beginning to fail and my oxygen level was decreasing. One more treatment and I'd have been on the iron lung!"

Rowdy never saw him again, but he'd heard what he needed to

hear.

"It was like [the technician] was an angel. Even though he never came back, I remember every detail of his face. That night, I started doing whatever I could to fight. I needed to stop feeling sorry for myself. I started telling the doctors I was willing to do whatever it took to get better."

It's one of those ideas that sounds good on paper, though it's hard to put into action.

Consider that Rowdy was almost completely paralyzed. He couldn't eat because his jaw wouldn't go all the way down. And when he talked, he was unable to fully articulate all he was trying to communicate. But, by continuing to go through the arduous process that was plasmapheresis every other day, within about four weeks' time, he started showing some signs of improvement.

"I never thought of dying," Rowdy says, a little matter-of-factly. "I never thought I was going to die, not once." After some studying up on the disease or syndrome, he learned many were able to manage a full recovery. There was his hope; that was his glass half full. He definitely had the intent of regaining his health but, with how long it was taking, his patience started wearing thin. He started feeling sorry for himself again.

Fortunately, his friend, Dru Dunworth – someone who was suffering from cancer and Hodgkin's disease simultaneously – was able to bring the Olympian back around. He told him to get his act together, that he was going to be just fine. And that was another motivation, one Rowdy desperately needed in order to push through.

He got there.

The news program *Hard Copy* and others reported the plight of a man who had captivated international attention not so long before. And letters from fans began to arrive.

"There were too many cards to respond to, literally thousands," Judy said. "But we read each one as we sat in the hospital. Grateful for the love and support that we felt."

Rowdy had to learn how to walk again. He had to learn how to swim again. But, as hard as those things were for him, he had a new lease on life. He willed himself into getting healthier and better, returning to the version of the man he once was. If he hadn't been the very regular swimmer he was, if he had not been continually striving to reach new personal best times all the while, the reality is he may not have pulled through. His dedication to the sport was a literal lifesaver.

"My neurologist actually told me, 'If you were not a swimmer, and you were not in the kind of shape you were in when you came in,

I'm not telling you you would have died, but you would have been put on the iron lung.' And that saved me a lot of heartache."

Judy recalls helping him get up to go to the bathroom one afternoon and having him faint before they made it there. He was out cold. There she was, stuck against the tile and absolutely helpless before others arrived to carry him back to his bed. Smelling salts brought him to his senses and he promptly broke out into a full body sweat. It was determined on the spot that they weren't going to allow him to get up anymore, whether he was being assisted or not. It was far too dangerous.

Based on that experience and his relapsing three more times after being released from the hospital, Judy couldn't help but worry about him constantly. And, when he got healthier and started back in with his normal routines again, she didn't necessarily stop.

The fear remained that something might still happen, that he might relapse yet again. A few months later, he was on an airplane and back to work when he passed out inside the plane's bathroom. When he woke up, he had no idea what had happened. He didn't even know how long he'd been there. Stories like that are reasons why Judy's concern never totally vanished.

"I thought, what if he falls and hits his head? I wouldn't be there to take care of him."

When he was finally released from the hospital, he didn't go straight home. He had one place he wanted to go, in spite of the fact it'd been advised against by the medical staff: He wanted to go to the Oahu Club. It had a pool attached to it and he wanted to get back in the water. It wasn't really a question of whether it would happen or not, but how soon.

Rowdy had lost a considerable amount of weight during his stay — about fifty pounds — and was a mere shadow of the man he was just weeks previous. It caused a woman familiar with the athlete to burst out crying once he arrived at the club; she even said he looked like a starved refugee. Not that it deterred him.

He was helped into the fifty-meters-long pool and, even though finishing a single lap was completely out of the question, he had to give it a shot. The desire was overwhelming. This is, after all, how he would heal.

The pool had once seemed so small to him. Today, it looked like the ocean. Not only did it appear endless, but it was intimidating. It was all Rowdy could do to stand in one spot and weakly move his arms around in small circles. The sight managed to break Judy's heart that much more.

She was all set to follow the doctor's orders and tried to keep Rowdy from swimming, but it didn't work out that way.

"And he's feeble and weak and barely able to stand and, there he is ... he's swimming," she said. "I thought he was going to drown."

Because he weighed "next to nothing," he was only about a foot under the top of the water. Not surprisingly, he wasn't moving at his usual pace, either. She could hardly even keep track of where he was most of the time.

"And then you'd see an arm slowly come out of the water, and then, a little bit later, another arm. And we were crying."

Once the world's fastest swimmer, Rowdy Gaines somehow managed his way across the fifty-meter pool that day. When he rose from those waters, the only thing Judy said she could see through her teary eyes was the huge smile on his face.

The pool was all he'd talked about at the hospital. In his mind, water was the solution. It cured everything. Because he has a strong emotional connection with the water, because it has served to relax him in almost all tense or horrific situations he's ever been part of, this was how he meditated.

Rowdy had done some of the rehabilitation exercises, but he knew water would be his real therapy. It's the longest he'd been out of the water since he was a young boy in Winter Haven. Yes, he had to relearn how to swim, but he got there.

"I was the third kid when I got home. I couldn't even pick up my own children. And when your two-year-old runs into your arms and you can't pick her up, that's tough."

Judy was on hand to help teach him how to swim. All at once, the teacher became the student.

"He's got that iron will, you know? When he came back from the pool that day, he said he was so happy. It was all he wanted to do."

Six months later, Rowdy was healthy again. He'd conquered the disease and the odds and could swim. Again. And, not only that, but he could swim very, very well. Having gained his weight back, he felt as normal as he had before he contracted Guillain-Barre. And, one year to the month, he went to the Masters World Championships in Indianapolis and won the 50- and 100-meter events in his age group.

Postscript

Never take your health for granted. It's such an easy thing for a healthy person to do. We don't think about getting sick. I've a great appreciation for what God has given me. Whether you believe in Him or not, you have to admit that the human body is a pretty amazing thing. So many things can go wrong. I learned to appreciate my health. Not in a weird way, but I know it was a gift that's been given me. So I am trying to do what's right with it. I'm doing my best to take care of myself.

Swimming might have saved my life physically but there is no doubt that Judy saved my life emotionally. There were many days I was ready to give up and she never let me. Not only was she taking care of our six- and two-year-old at home but she was holding me together for three months at the hospital and the many months of recovery at home afterwards. To this day I don't know how she was able to do it but I will be eternally grateful for her being there for me then and now.

Swimming was an essential part of

finding the motivation to stay alive. Because I know where my body was at the time and I know my body was completely shutting down. I could feel everything starting to go. It's a scary thought, being that near to death. I felt that. I was very close to being in bad shape. When it was all said and done, because of my lung capacity and the shape I was in, it saved me a lot of heartache, if not my life. I've got nothing but gratitude to the sport for that.

I have no effects today, except for a tingling in my fingers and toes that has never gone away. I can feel that right now even. When it's cold, I become a bit arthritic. I get cold easily. Otherwise? I've made a 100 percent recovery. I have never looked back.

—Rowdy Gaines

Adversity has the ability to cause you

to reflect upon your blessings and help to define the things that are most important to you. This was a very humbling experience that we shared together and we became stronger as a couple because of it.

We learned that family is the most important thing to us and to never take your health for granted. We learned that there truly are angels who walk upon the Earth seen and unseen in the form of friends, family, and medical professionals. And we learned they will come to your aid and in your time of need.

—Judy Gaines

Not a Retiring Guy

Nobody gives awards for swimming around the world more than two or three times. If they did, they'd have to pass that award Rowdy's way. When he was training for the Olympics, someone determined he swam about 20,000 miles – approximately the circumference of the globe. Since that time, he's done at least that many miles and more. With the wear and tear of thousands of miles in the swim lane over the past four decades, an obvious question presents itself: When will it actually stop?

When you ask Rowdy when it is that he'll finally hang up his trunks and quit with the swimming for good, he almost takes offense to even being asked. He twists up his face and wastes no time firing an answer back in your direction, one it appears he's had prepared for a while. He's a man with his mind made up.

"When they bury me six feet under," he says immediately. "I'll never stop swimming. No way, not possible, never ever."

And he's quick to add: "I constantly crave it. It's a borderline obsession for me."

Anyone who's witnessed him being unable to swim at least once every day or two knows that's the truth. Keep him out of the water for a couple of days and he transforms from his congenial, approachable self to an agitated guy you don't much want to be around.

This decision to keep swimming comes after he's already more or less retired three times. Rowdy had his reasons to do so too, each one different from the next.

There was the time he was still a senior in college, where he was on scholarship at Auburn and the captain of the swim team. Rowdy had survived an Olympic boycott of the Games he had been expected to dominate and wasn't altogether certain the entire movement wouldn't vanish completely, leaving him without his lifelong goal of attaining at least one gold medal. It was all but gone. At one point, there was even talk of replacing the Olympics with something called the Goodwill Games. The political ramifications put doubts in people's minds about whether or not the Olympics could happen as it had before.

"We didn't want politics at the Olympics," Rowdy says. "We just wanted something the whole world would want to come to."

But it was more complex than that. Graduation was right around the corner, which would mean he'd no longer have access to trainers whenever he wanted help. And being treated like a prince on campus would become a luxury of the past. Retiring at this point simply amounted to leaping toward that next stepping stone, whatever it was. And he didn't know where that leap would take him. He just felt it was necessary.

"I had to go back to the real world," he remarks. "I was graduating from college and there was no money in swimming in 1981. Everyone did that. Everyone 'retired,' so to speak. I had to give up this fantasy world and think about what I was going to do to earn a living.

"I had to come back down to earth and quit living in the clouds. Besides, I knew it couldn't last forever."

And so, at twenty-two, Rowdy retired to begin his short-lived career as a lifeguard. He even had time to party with his friends and hang out, like any other normal young adult. Gone was the grind of training day in and day out: It was as welcome a break as it was a brief one. When all you're doing is sitting on a big stool and watching "snotty-nosed" kids run around all day, you've a lot of time left to your own thoughts. In fact, it's what he did all summer long, whether he wanted to or not: He thought a lot.

His feelings of uncertainty and trepidation ran rampant. What if he trained for the next three years of his life, only to have the rug pulled out from under him again? What if the Olympics never happened for him once again? Was it worth the long hours of devotion to his sport if it was going to essentially blow up in his face? And was there any way around repeating that scenario? Could he protect himself from that kind of heartbreak?

A conversation with his father, Buddy, helped redirect that train of thought. As much as he was uncertain about returning to the water, there was another side of him that wanted nothing more than to do just that – to do what it was he hadn't been able to yet. He'd broken his share of records (throughout the world and otherwise), but there was a level he hadn't reached and it was one he aspired to. Fortunately his dad understood that, perhaps better than even Rowdy did.

He asked his son a simple question.

"How long do you want to live?" he asked, to which a clearly perplexed Rowdy answered, "I don't know … eighty? Eighty-five? Ninety, maybe?"

He wasn't real sure what his dad was attempting to get across.

> *"So you're going to live for another sixty years. And you don't want to sacrifice another three years out of your life for something you've dreamt about all your life? You do that and you're going to have to look in the mirror and have doubts from here on out."*

He had a point. Already, Rowdy felt an emptiness and real sense of regret whenever he saw a flash of the Olympic rings on television. Tied to that, every single time he came across some tidbit about swimming, that dull ache returned.

Long story short? The retirement wasn't a very long one. It lasted from March to September of 1981. It didn't take very long before he was back in the water, every single day, having regained the same drive and fervor that had placed him on the team in 1980.

It's said amongst serious swimmers that, for every day you're actually out of the water, it takes half a day to get the feeling of the water back again. Because Rowdy had been out for six months, he knew he had three months to get back to where he once was.

"And there was a lot of pain when I got back in the pool. At least with running, you're used to walking all the time. You're doing the things you'd do naturally," he says. "But if you don't swim, you lose that natural motion of the water that your body gets used to when you swim every day."

This wasn't the first time Rowdy had retired, changed his mind, then returned to the pool. The first time, he was just nine years old when he'd decided he'd had it.

He'd been on the Cypress Gardens swim team two summers when he decided he'd set his sights on the greener pastures of, oh, the Little League teams he'd not been able to try out for because he'd been practicing so much. It was easy to understand why, too, as he was afforded very few luxuries. Back then, nobody on his swim team even had a pair of goggles. To add to that, the water was far too cold for his liking in the winter months. Just like that, he was done.

It's readily understood that true-blooded Floridians don't really get in the water from October until May. According to Rowdy, it's one way to tell the tourists from the locals: There's just no use swimming when the water's far too cold to do so.

So he closed that chapter and went back to being a carefree kid … at least for a bit.

His other retirement — his third — came the very year he made a clean sweep at the 1984 Olympic Games. He submitted his retirement papers to USA Swimming and was taken off his routine drug testing. It was the only way for him to retrieve any monies owed him by the governing body of the sport. He had done appearances leading up to the Olympics and accrued his share of sponsorship money, but he couldn't keep anything outside of what he needed for personal living expenses. Retiring allowed him to withdraw the sum in its entirety. With that act, he essentially forced himself into retirement. Of the three times he chose to surrender his sport, he had the least say in the matter this time around. He could have submitted his papers again and even competed again, but why? The way he saw it, he had finally accomplished the goal that had driven him for so many years. He didn't need to do any more than he'd already done.

Or, at least, it seemed that way at first. When he was offered a trip to Australia in 1988 by a man named Tiger Holmes, it changed some things for him.

"He offered to fly me to Australia if I competed in the Masters meet there. I thought, hmm, free trip to Australia? Okay!"

Incidentally, Holmes is a longtime swimming advocate who has remained connected with Rowdy for years. Even at the age of ninety-three in 2014, Holmes broke a world record at the Masters swim meet named in honor of the very athlete he had recruited to compete in

Australia all those years ago.

The swimming and the training were back on. After a few races, Rowdy ended up almost accidentally qualifying for the Olympic trials in 1988. He wasn't completely serious about it and it wasn't as if he'd made an eighteen-month comeback of any kind. In fact, he was only swimming once a day. His aspirations, if he had any at that point, were modest at best.

Rowdy came in seventh in the 100 Free, but they only accepted the top six qualifiers. He came close, as close as he possibly could have, but it wasn't enough. In fact, he missed out on going to the Olympics again by three-hundredths of a second. It was something that hurt his pride, especially when he came as close as he did.

He got over that hiccup. He was able to discover a renewed love for swimming. It's led to his breaking more than thirty world records since, having become a vibrant part of the Masters swimming community. He swims less than he once did — an hour during his lunch breaks compared to the six hours a day he used to do — but that too has its benefits.

"Starting to swim again and winning again, that was rewarding. Was it redemption? No. But was it rewarding? Oh, yeah."

Postscript

A lot of people will make fun of athletes that come out of retirement and try to make comebacks. I feel just the opposite. If they want to come back and do something they have a passion for, by all means, do it. The only problem I have is when they're putting their lives in danger.

Janet Evans made a comeback when she was 41 years old. People are asking why; why doesn't she just stay retired? It's none of their business. You should always do what you love. You should always follow that path. Sometimes that passion is hard to maintain day in and day out and it will dissipate so much that you do want to quit, but it can be rekindled too. I was and always have been a huge fan of Janet when she was winning gold at 16 in 1988. Even though it didn't work out with her comeback in 2012, I was so proud of the attempt.

I look at swimmers trying to make a comeback with adulation and amazement. I would come back right now if I could do it.

—Rowdy Gaines

Up Close, Personal

Rowdy's rise from a small Florida high school into the historic ranks of world-class swimmers is only part of his story. What happened out of the public eye has been a quiet determinant in helping mold him into an international ambassador for the sport.

The humble, driven athlete rose to stardom in his youth and managed to attract some superstars along the way. He once dated supermodel Cindy Crawford and spent time with Joan Jett. The spotlight liaisons didn't last but at least one of them had some lasting effects on him. Ultimately, he met an attractive young half-Italian woman who stole his heart and helped him build the life he has led for the last thirty-plus years.

Stardust

It seems a far-fetched tall tale to learn Rowdy once became fast friends with Joan Jett. To most, the two go together as well as mismatched socks. She's quick to recognize that. "The two images don't quite mesh, Rowdy and me," Joan said during an interview. "That's because I'm weird. But it was a really fantastic time."

One snapshot from the mid-1980s more or less tells the thousand words he remains relatively tight-lipped about. There she is, at the height of her glory, riding high on her fame as singer and leader of the Blackhearts. And, there he is, a likely unknown in any of the same circles, next to her and beaming. And why shouldn't he be?

If the photo could speak, maybe it would describe how they were two kids who ran into one another at a concert for a few hundred athletes. She had been chosen to perform at the Olympic Village in Los Angeles, where he and his compatriots got what amounted to an intimate club show. He was riding high on his American win, a few gold medals attached to his name. There were other performers there, too, Bruce Springsteen and Lionel Richie among them. But it was Joan who captivated Rowdy's attention.

It's been a bit since that all took place and Rowdy is quick to back out of his words, saying she probably won't even consider their time together as any kind of relationship, per se. But few can say they dated a singer in a band (and a rather well-known one at that). Even fewer can say they had the chance to hang out in New York City with a rock legend, and regularly at that.

Concerts were happening every night of the Olympics, sixteen in all. And because swimming always happens during the first eight days of the Games, Rowdy didn't get to see a single performance. He was in shutdown mode, totally focused. He considered no diversions.

As for those second eight days, it was time for Rowdy and his friends to have some fun.

The long-established athlete and the rock legend (along with her manager) offer different perspectives of the night the two rising stars met.

"The night after I won, Joan performed in the Village. She was very popular and I, like pretty much anybody else at the time, loved Joan Jett," Rowdy said. "I thought she was awesome. She played for about an hour, even came out to sign autographs and take photos."

Kenny Laguna, longtime manager for Joan, still remembers that night.

"Rowdy and a couple guys from the swimming team came over and they were very gregarious, not shy or standoffish in the least," Laguna recalls. There were no reporters or public mixed in with the athletes. The band had just played in Panama before traveling to Los

Angeles to perform, he says.

The Olympian was able to strike up a conversation with Joan as she had just seen him swim.

For Joan, he represented the best of what America was putting forth in the international competition.

"Rowdy had had a great Olympics and we were pulling for the American team, of course," she said. "It was cool being in the middle of that whole experience and meeting this down-to-earth, friendly guy."

"It was such an overwhelming experience for me and I'm sure for the athletes as well. I'm a closet jock. I always watched the Olympics, so it was very exciting for me to be playing for them, period ... a high honor."

An easy friendship was formed. After the Olympics, it was dinners in New York City whenever he'd come around. And there were concerts. Considering the era, it meant seeing Billy Idol and Cyndi Lauper and even U2. Rowdy and Joan even met and hung out with Peter Frampton once. One thing they never did, though — they never played a single one of her records.

"We never listened to her music, not once," he said. "She didn't like it. She was embarrassed. I'd want her to turn it on and sing, but she never did."

Joan Jett and Rowdy became friends in '84 (top) and met again in 2014.

Her stage persona as a rebel belied the fact she was "very sweet, very kind and very shy too."

Joan, for her part, knows the power of a first impression. And meeting Rowdy meant an immediate connection, a welcomed one that's lasted far beyond those Games. She characterized the lasting nature of their friendship.

"It's kind of hard to explain, or maybe it's very easy too," she says, on the phone from her native New York. "Everybody has a few people they meet in their lives who they get along with right away, almost like you already know them. It was that kind of comfort level. I'm not sure how much that had to do with what Rowdy and I were doing at the time, both of us being very successful and being able to relate. We're very different, sports and rock and roll, but there are a lot of similarities."

"And then there was my wanting to be an athlete, so I asked a million questions. He was one of those guys I immediately liked and felt comfortable around, which says a lot. You can become very untrusting with people in this business, so to get that sense and be proved right on it, that's great. It's nice to still have that bond."

It's a friendship that means he and a couple of his friends are invited to stand on the stage with Joan and her band when she performs for a rabid crowd at Busch Gardens in Tampa, Florida. It's a friendship that warrants her dropping his name between songs and reminiscing with the crowd about some of that time gone by.

There's some time spent in her trailer after the concert and some catching up, as the friends haven't seen one another in what might be two decades. Smiles and stories and memories abound.

Rowdy, for his part, feels he knows why that kind of friendship still exists.

"Part of the connection is that we still love what we do. I still love swimming and Joan still loves rock and roll," he says. "Maybe that's the conduit, the connection: that we appreciate each other for what we've done for our respective careers."

Joan senses a similar connectivity.

"Both of the things we do are pretty physical," she adds. "He travels as much or more than me, doing meets and training and announcing. It's really a testament to his willpower and love for what he does. And I love what I do and that I'm still blessed to be able to do it. There is definitely a parallel."

Gravitational pull

Even though Joan Jett made a lasting impression on Rowdy, it was another relationship that managed to reshape his life. If he'd not met his wife of 28 years when he did – and at a gas station no less – he would not have the life he enjoys today. Meeting Judy helped him transition from being absolutely consumed with his performance in the pool to being the father of four girls while he led and motivated countless others.

It makes sense that Rowdy is the product of parents who started out as water ski performers and also that his seventy-seven-year-old father resides on an island in southwestern Florida off the Gulf of Mexico. He collects shark's teeth by the handfuls every day and swims in the ocean with his wife of thirty-plus years as much as he sees fit.

But what of the other family, his wife and their four daughters? With an address in a gated community north of Orlando, Florida, he cuts through any thought of pretensions and jokingly compares his family to the Clampetts in the old television sitcom *The Beverly Hillbillies*.

"That's just the silliness of us," he says. "We're just a bunch of hicks sitting down and talking about the good old times. We make fun of ourselves."

Barring that, the man can't seem to get those he's so connected to off his mind.

"I'm obsessed with my kids," he admits. "I can't think of anything else I'd want to do but be with them." He pauses to allow that to sink in a second. "It's kinda sick."

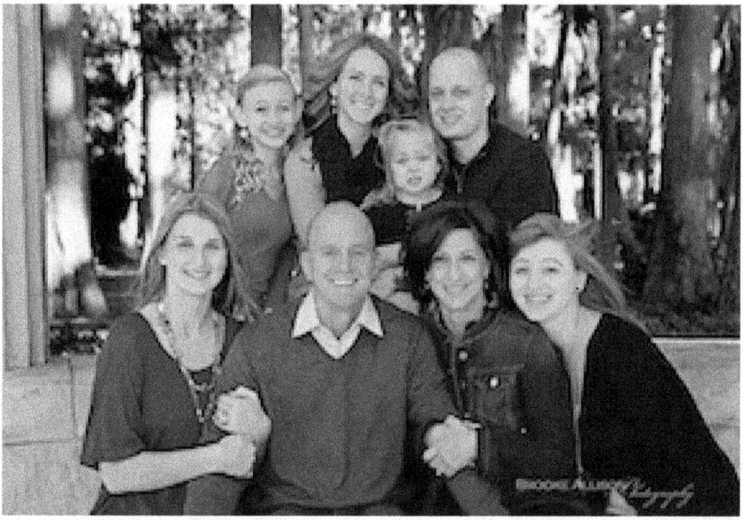

Family members include, left to right: Savanna, Rowdy, Judy and Madison Gaines (bottom row); Isabelle Gaines, Emily Henrie, Bella Henrie, Tyrone Henrie (top row).

And so it's the easiest thing in the world for him to carve out a hole in his schedule when his youngest daughter Isabelle once does a report on her Olympian daddy for her sixth-grade class ("He just talked about himself the whole time," she deadpans). And he easily gets talked into bringing a not-so-unexpected prize home from work when one of his kids stays home sick from school.

Swimming and family are it. Nothing else matters. And, while he'll be the first to admit that sort of behavior might qualify the Gaines family as some of the most boring suburbanites, there's no reason to change. Rowdy flat out loves his family.

"There is no way you can deny that," he says. "They are the reasons why I take red eyes coming home from a swimming clinic thousands of miles away and schedule the last possible flight out to go there, why I'm constantly looking at my watch at five o'clock and counting down to when I can be with them again."

Often on the national and international stage commentating or taking on the role as swim ambassador, Rowdy says he prefers sitting with his grandkids and watching *Spongebob Squarepants* on television, rubbing his daughter's feet or grilling a burger with his wife. He jokes that he would have no trouble being a "house husband."

And how about that near future? What of it? Here's one scenario:

"In ten years, I want to retire, buy an RV and travel the country visiting our grandchildren. We already have two. I just want to get to a point where we can do things together, doing everything we've never been able to."

As an athlete and father who's honed his talent to swim for most of his life, it stands to reason that some of his children might want to tap into some of that natural skill.

Then again, maybe not.

"[My daughter] Madison once looked me directly in the eye and said she'd rather eat dirt than swim," Rowdy says. "But I've never made any of them swim. There are times I wished I had, but, for the most part, I'm happy I didn't."

And, when it comes right down to it, having a family ranks higher for him than winning a race. Helping create an individual doesn't involve much in the way of winning – you don't necessarily win a thing – but it's still much more important, he says. Look at things that way and Olympics medals tend to pale in comparison.

Still, all he's learned as a result of his long career of swimming apply as a father: You still have to be dedicated, have teamwork, set goals, adhere to your responsibilities and, above all, be committed. These are lessons he'll never rid himself of.

Somewhere along the line, all of his girls have dabbled with swimming, though none have taken it anywhere close to the level he has. And he's certain that, with the right amount of dedication, they'd have risen to the top. But no one wants to be labeled as Rowdy Gaines' kid either.

Nobody wants to have to stand in the shadow of their father

and be compared to all the accomplishments he's been able to attach his name to. There's being fast and then there's being as fast as your dad. There's being good in the water and there's being as good in the water as your dad was.

"Deep inside, I would want them to swim. I love swimming. I love the lessons I learned. I love being in shape. And, for health purposes, I wanted them to do it. But I also know how hard it is. I didn't want to see them suffer. I was skittish about them going through the practices I did."

He refuses to give up hope entirely. His youngest talks about it all the time. Considering he didn't really start to make a name for himself until he was seventeen (she's still a teenager herself), does he keep a torch burning for her possible future? Why not? Perhaps there will be another swimmer in the family yet.

Still, if history is to teach anything, it will let on there weren't a lot of relatives who made it to the Olympics together, either simultaneously or otherwise. Gary Hall Sr. and Gary Hall Jr. were father and son swimmers, respectively, the son ending up with ten Olympic medals between 1996, 2000 and 2004. But it's rarer than it is common.

That's not to say that it can't still happen.

Medals

Throughout the backstage parties with Joan Jett, the courting of the woman who would become his life partner, and raising his daughters, three things remained a constant: His three gold medals.

His medals have practically earned a reputation of their own. They have risen above expectations on account of the man who won them in the first place.

When Rowdy was traveling through Saudi Arabia in 1985, an Olympian with a gold medal in his pocket, he wasn't rewarded with any kind of admiration. He did garner some attention, though: Several armed airport security guards strip-searched him.

They escorted him into a small room, asked him to remove all his clothes and watched to make certain he did. He sat there, completely naked, officials pummeling him with questions. Beyond the humiliation of being undressed, they didn't speak his language and he didn't speak theirs. It took some time to hurdle that communication barrier. For someone so normally unflappable, he was at a bit of a loss.

To be fair, this was more than fifteen years before airport security increased the world over in the wake of the 9/11 attack.

Aggressive screenings were rare. In fact, Rowdy had never experienced one during all of his international travels.

"So I'm in there with nothing on and my hands over my crotch. At the same time, I wasn't too worried. I just hadn't done anything wrong," he recalls. "I kept thinking to myself, 'I can explain my way out of this one.'"

Thirty confusing minutes later, the premonition proved right. He was given permission to get dressed and released.

And so it goes with the lives his three medals have lived along with him, each with stories of its own. While they were promptly given away to the very people who'd inspired him all along his storied path, they've gone on to be gawked at, passed around, complimented, rubbed on, stolen, returned, dropped, dinged, and lost. While his medals are each symbols of some of his loftiest accomplishments, he's not as attached to them as one might think.

"I've never been infatuated with the 'metal' part of the medals," he lets on. Since his coach Richard Quick passed away, he's retrieved one solitary gold medal to show the boys and girls he meets and teaches at swimming clinics. Since 1984, though, the ribbon's broken off. That medal was even stolen and returned to him in an unmarked envelope two months later. Once it found its way into the hands of a thief who thought it'd be a great idea to hold the thing for ransom. Fortunately, it was returned, without Rowdy paying a single cent. Whenever it has turned up missing, it has always made its way back to Rowdy.

Some Olympians have donated their medals to museums and others have opted to stash theirs away in safety deposit boxes. Some take them out on the road, where they're able to add a "show and tell" portion to their speaking engagements.

For Rowdy, he eventually learned how he should use the souvenir of his life's work.

"Three years after the '84 Olympics, my wife and I got to go to the Super Bowl and sit next to (football legend) Franco Harris. He had this amazing Super Bowl ring on that he took off and passed around all over the place, up and down the rows."

And the light bulb flashed on: Rowdy had an idea. He wondered, if he were to start travelling around the country with his medal in tow, would people benefit from it in some way? What if they had never seen one before? Shouldn't they be allowed that opportunity? The decision was made.

"The response was unbelievable! Now I'm able to put a smile on a kid's face and explain the history of the medals. I'm able to educate on events that have a 120-year-old legacy attached to them."

To look at the medal the kids eventually see, the one that gets pulled out of his pocket in an elementary school or swim clinic, it's seen its shinier days. It's pretty beat up. The gold has started rubbing off, as thousands upon thousands of hands have touched it and it's been dropped an estimated million times or so. There are nicks all over the medal, too. Along the side, the 1984 Olympics were once on proud display marking the event, but now? You can just barely make out those words.

"But I don't care about all that," he says, flatly. "The medal has weathered along with me."

There's an easy parallel to make here, between this heavy circle of battered gold and the man who admits he used to keep it in his kitchen drawer at home: Both still persevere, even though neither may really be entirely what it once was.

When others marvel at the impossibility of a gold medal, they don't necessarily care that it's not as shiny new as it was all those many years ago, but that it was achieved and how. It's about the journey.

Postscript

The kids who are the most shy are the ones I'm drawn to. I can sense somebody in pain. Usually, at the end of one of my clinics, I have my medal and, instead of passing it around, I choose a kid to hold it for me while others come up and touch it. If I can't find the right kid, I always ask the coach to pick the one who is the single best kid he knows. Not the best swimmer, but the one with the best disposition and44 attitude. They love it. They absolutely love it. All of a sudden, they're the most popular ones there for those few minutes.

Two specific moments in my post-Olympic career helped me put what I did in perspective. The day after I won my last gold medal, my coach woke me up at six in the morning and drove me to a children's hospital in Los Angeles. He told me we were going to visit some sick children. He said that what I had done was fantastic and that it was something I should be very proud of. But, at the end of the day, it was just a swim race and there are a lot more important things in life than that. He wanted me to appreciate the gift I'd been given and said that a lot of people would never have that gift. We spent the whole morning with a lot of really cool children, most who were terminally ill. It was eye-opening. It brought me down to earth in a hurry.

As for that other moment, it was when I went to Sandy Hook, exactly one year after that tragic shooting had taken place. My daughter Emily wanted to do something for those families. I found the coach there and offered to visit and do a free swim clinic. I remember doing the clinic and meeting one of the little girls on the swim team; her brother (who had also been on the team) had been shot and killed during that tragedy. And I got her to smile. Her father came up to me after and was in tears. He said it was the first time he'd seen her smile since her brother had died.

So is there a bigger purpose than just swimming two laps in a pool and winning a race? Yes, there most certainly is.

When I speak to a group of children, I am sure to tell every one of them they have a gift inside; they just may not know what it is yet. That gift might be the gift of swimming and it might mean something else. People are too quick to say you're worthless and you're not talented, but I don't believe that. I believe every single kid has something that they can excel at. It's a matter of exploring and nurturing and testing and practicing and repeating to find it. Some might never discover what it is, but it's there.

—Rowdy Gaines

Mastering the Masters

There's a poorly kept secret to attach to the world of swimming. It's so poorly kept that over 70,000 swimmers across the United States and some 200,000-plus swimmers in Japan know about it. It includes teamwork, exercise, competition, even a strong sense of family. It's a way to keep skills up and break world records and perfect that butterfly when you're pushing ninety years of age.

The not-so-secret secret is the world of Masters swimming, an organized program of swimming for adults. U.S. Masters Swimming has been around since 1970 and is a nonprofit membership national governing body.

Rowdy devotes himself to Masters swimming. He's held a Masters competition at the YMCA Aquatic Center in Orlando for more than seven years, and breaking records for each of those events has practically become an expected norm. In 2015, the event that bears his name welcomed over 400 swimmers.

For him, Masters is a place where who you are and how good your stroke is aren't the most important reasons to take part. There's more to it. In fact, he refers to the Masters world as an "anti-aging miracle."

"It's the fountain of youth," Rowdy says. "You're able to stay in shape and do it in a structured way. You can be around people who feel the same way you do about swimming."

"You can do it at any age, no matter how old you get. And that sure beats taking medication."

Little wonder then that the number of Masters swimmers grows as regularly as it does; the list of ongoing benefits is a long one. Participating helps lower blood pressure. It eliminates bad cholesterol. It strengthens the immune system and helps minimize chronic pain. It's why both experienced and inexperienced swimmers show up in their suits and swim just as fast — or as steady and slowly — as they want to go. Even if they don't win their races, they feel pretty good after.

Rowdy tackles the Masters with much of the same fervor and talent he displayed early in his career. In 2010, he and his handpicked team of seasoned swimmer friends broke a world record in their age group for swimming the fastest. It marked a particularly high point for the crowd at the Second Annual Rowdy Gaines Classic.

And, for the lone Olympian of the group, having been able to accomplish that kind of achievement in a relay setting was particularly significant as the team shared equally in the success.

"To be able to share that with guys who would never have had that chance, that was the most meaningful part for me," Rowdy says of the event. "Just think about the guys we had on the team: a former high school swimmer, a fifty-nine-year-old TV broadcaster, an insurance executive, a guy who owns his own pool cleaning company. To be able to do that with them was beyond special. It was the reason I did it, period."

It wasn't his first time to break a world record for speed. The first time he did so he was twenty six years old, when FINA (International Swimming Federation) named him the fastest swimmer on the planet. In fact, he's broken more than thirty world speed records, though he doesn't appear to care about tracking the actual total.

Continuing to progress is an important driver for him. If his only competition is the Rowdy Gaines from a year back, he wants to put that guy behind him, no matter how fast he was. Take one of the recent Nationals events he's been training to compete in on the other side of the nation, for example. He's in full-on training mode, wide-eyed and excited, borrowing his habits from a time gone by.

When he gets there on his first day, he'll take clippers to his head (along with shaving his arms, legs, and chest) but not a day before. The disciplines that took place in college and high school continue today.

"We'd let our hair grow the whole year, our beards too. Our hair would be all over the place," he recalls. "In the summertime, after we'd been swimming as much as we did, the chlorine was so bad, my hair would dry right out. I'd reach up and grab a piece and it would break off, just flat-out disintegrate."

Does going entirely hairless make him swim faster? That's up for debate. To every swimmer, there exists a certain grab bag of traditions and suspicions that never really goes away. This, then, remains one of his favorites, one of his go-tos.

With races determined on hundredths of a second, it doesn't hurt to stick with what helps give you the edge. Rowdy's competition would like nothing more than to beat a three-time Olympic gold medalist in the water, even if he earned his medals over thirty years ago. As nice as he seems, he's not going to allow that to happen.

"I may as well go out there and do my absolute best," he says, admitting to living on little more than energy bars for several days in a row. He refuses any offered baked goods within reach, his love of brownies notwithstanding. "I'm in training shape, so I may as well get after it. I want to swim fast. I always want to."

He comes back after the event having swum faster than he has in two years, beating his old record by a mere fraction of a second and managing to set a new speed record in his age bracket. He shares the good news with thousands of others through his Twitter and Facebook accounts, too. Whatever it was that allowed for it to happen, be it the total absence of hair or the steady ingestion of protein bars or day after day of rigorous swimming, it certainly appears to have worked in his favor.

Within that Masters group of tens of thousands of swimmers over the age of eighteen, Rowdy has often competed with a team of now-friends that he has acquired over the years. People like Scot Weiss, Marc Middleton, Keith Switzer and Charlie Lydecker, to name a few. Each was a pretty good swimmer in his youth, but each has become progressively better with age. None has any kind of Olympic glory to attach to their name. They simply came together when they were each in their fifties and Rowdy helped drive their collective success to new heights.

Middleton, who had swum very little since high school meets

more than forty years ago, was motivated to join the team primarily for the camaraderie with Rowdy.

"What he does, he does better than everybody," Middleton notes. "He has the ability to inspire you to want to do very well, but there is no pressure. Most are involved to have fun, to do good and to support their competitors. It's competing in the most positive way."

When people encounter Rowdy as he poses for photos, signs autographs and talks to strangers like they're his closest friends, Middleton says, they are inclined to think he's putting on some kind of a superficial front. He's not. The former sportscaster said his teammate acts the same way on a pool deck and helping run a meet of more than 2,000 competitors as he does one-on-one with friends. The only time he ever changes is when he's on the starting block, ready to race.

"He becomes some sort of savage beast and he's off. He owns a gear that nobody else has; he has a fifth or sixth gear when everybody else has four," says Middleton, who now oversees Growing Bolder, a media group aimed at promoting active lifestyles. "As soon as he finishes, as soon as he touches, that competitive look on his face fades away and he's back again."

If you catch Rowdy waxing philosophical about his participation in Masters Swimming, he's quick to acknowledge the other reasons he does it too.

"The competition is not as critical to me as it is staying in shape and being connected to people who are still athletic, people who feel healthy and largely are," he says. "When I go to a meet, I feel like part of a big family."

It's about living at the top of his game through a sport he has, yes, mastered. Inspiring others along the way is one of those built-in advantages.

"I like that when I go, some people look up to me in the water. I feel like I continue to inspire. That ability to do so is a pretty good feeling, regardless of how it comes. Knowing that I can do that for the rest of my life? That's one of those good feelings."

Rob Butcher, former executive director of Masters Swimming and now heading up Swim Across America, said Rowdy possesses a character trait that eludes so many former champions.

"He never said, 'I'm done with swimming and I need to go on with the rest of my life.' What's fascinating is that he hit the highest of highs and never went away from it," Butcher said. Attached to Masters Swimming for more than fifteen years, Butcher has swam in over 300 Masters relays and is a USMS certified coach. That's another way of saying, well, he speaks with a fair amount of authority.

Rowdy, Butcher said, has managed to hang onto his boyhood love of swimming.

"He's not lost that. And it's interesting, because he's hit the pinnacle of pinnacles," Butcher said. "But when he steps off the block, he's as warm as ever. It's part of his DNA, a natural high for him. He feeds off of them like they feed off of him."

What's more, he's been at it for so long, he can't be at a swimming pool without getting recognized instantly.

All his Olympic "brothers and sisters" know him well. When they see him still having fun at all he does, they're able to latch onto him as a role model. They can look up to him and keep swimming, he says.

It's sometimes difficult for Olympians to move on from the experience they had winning. The swimmers may come away from this monumental achievement having swum faster than anyone in front of a larger crowd than they'll ever see again. Matching that experience can seem more than daunting.

"The thing is, Rowdy has been able to internally replicate that feeling," Butcher says. "And with that he finds such internal joy."

Rowdy doesn't intend to stop anytime soon.

"Someday I will be in the eighty- to eighty-four-year-old age group, cranking against those others," Rowdy says. "I'll be swimming until they bury me and put me six feet under."

Just how well does Rowdy stack up against the others? At one time, he held every single freestyle world record in his age group, something that had never been done before in his sport.

Despite the prestige the records have brought with them, he's always known he stood to lose them, and at any given time too. World records are made to be broken.

"I'm not knocking the feeling – breaking a world record is exhilarating – but I'd trade 100 world records for one gold medal. That gold doesn't go away. The medal – the medals – are mine. They always will be."

Twenty Years Calling Olympics

If you've listened to or watched an Olympic swim race over the last twenty years, you've heard Rowdy's excited voice. The story of his broadcasting evolution, from commentating for pay-per-view stations to providing insight and perspective for NBC Olympics, reflects the tenacity he showed during his career in the pool. And a good portion of his journey has taken place outside the swimming pool, with an even longer career as a broadcaster.

His love for swimming hasn't been pushed to the wayside – he's a stone's throw away from a swim race at any given time – he's simply shifted toward describing and commentating on new and seasoned swimmers making headlines of their own. Though it wasn't necessarily his goal at first, he's earned a new audience by doing so. He's able to talk about and discuss swimming on television in a way few before him have.

When Michael Phelps earned eight gold medals in Beijing in

2008, Rowdy was on the edge of his seat and describing every detail to a worldwide audience as history unfolded. When Misty Hyman managed in 2000 to surprise Rowdy and others by winning the women's 200-meter butterfly in Sydney, Rowdy was beside himself and screaming for the woman who was practically disregarded as an underdog. And when Summer Sanders won that same race in 1992 in her final chance at winning gold (and Rowdy's first Olympics as a commentator), he was on hand to help share that news with context and insight.

The list of events he's been part of is ever-growing. And given his long history of calling races for an audience of millions, there's probably been more unsaid than said and plenty not seen by the public eye or openly discussed. Nobody's going to ask Rowdy what he does in between takes, when the cameras are pointing other directions. These are some of those highlights that viewers have missed but ones Rowdy nevertheless remembers.

The guidelines to being a good color analyst or anchor can be challenging.

All of the on-air talent must remain neutral when talking about the athletes competing — even when the contenders are favorites back home, unsung American heroes or rising stars from U.S. soil. It's something Rowdy gets reminded of every four years when NBC holds its Olympic seminar for all involved. Producers, directors, and commentators are not to refer to the Americans as "we," but refer to them as Americans and little more. It's not the easiest task. It's something Rowdy had to get used to, especially considering it's the American swimmers he generally knows the most about. It's safe to say the former American team member considers the U.S. team as his very own.

"Have I ever referred to a swimmer as 'we' during a broadcast?" he asks aloud, trying to remember. "No, I haven't. But I have been tempted."

Another guideline: When an athlete is injured or even seems to have an issue, commentators are never to assume a thing (especially because they're the ones sitting closest to the microphones). They pretty much have to hold their breath along with everyone else until a sideline reporter confirms what actually took place. It saves them from apologizing later for accidentally misinforming viewers.

Jim McKay is the Olympic anchor Rowdy remembers best, both because he hosted twelve Olympic Games and because he interviewed Rowdy after his wins in 1984. Rowdy calls him the "gentle grandfather" who brought the Olympics into people's homes each night. Bob Costas was able to continue that tradition of excellence over the past twenty-plus years. Rowdy's been honored to be a color analyst for the past six Games and counting (Rio will be his seventh). While he's not completely involved when it comes to discussing the technical aspects of swimming, his specialty is sharing the reasons why and how something is happening. It's something he's grown into over time, to the point it seems almost second nature for him.

"I think the main reason I am able to continue doing what I do, year in and year out, is no one can deny my passion for the sport," he says. "That comes across to the TV watcher at home."

Broadcasting the Olympics requires more dedication and preparation than most viewers realize. For example, Costas all but locks himself in a room for a solid week before any given Olympics so he can study details such as the competitors, the venue and any new rules. Rowdy usually gets to the Games two weeks before they begin, to immerse himself in similar details. By the time competition begins, Rowdy and his fellow broadcasters know more about the athletes then the competitors know about themselves.

"[Five-time Olympic medalist] John Naber taught me that we are not the story. We are reporting the story," he says. "It's advice I like so much, I return and adhere to it, over and over again."

1992 — Barcelona

In 1992, Rowdy announced for what was then called a triplecast. Considered ahead of its time more than two decades ago, three pay-per-view stations were on twenty-four hours a day. And each of the three channels broadcast a different sport. Viewers could watch live, in real time, whenever they wanted. It was his first experience in Olympic broadcasting and he was calling every single race. Calling the events without the safety net of being recorded was stressful but it gave him his first chance at relaying the excitement of the Games to viewers. It's where he began to hone his broadcasting skills. Doing so allowed him to learn something important in fairly short order: He absolutely loved it. And he didn't have to force himself; he was a natural.

It made for an especially memorable time as it was his first opportunity to meet O.J. Simpson, another brand new broadcaster. At least to Rowdy, there were no hints of character flaws in Simpson, who would later be tried and acquitted of murdering his former wife in 1994.

"He couldn't have been nicer. He was very inquisitive about

Olympic swimming and asking all about Summer Sanders and Pablo Morales and what they were like and on and on. He was genuinely interested in the sport," Rowdy recalls. "Little did I know that, just a year later, he'd go off the deep end."

Rowdy cried during these Olympics; he had tears falling down his cheeks for the first of three times while he was on the air. Never one to bury his emotions too far below the surface, he still managed to surprise himself when it actually happened. The first time, it was when Pablo Morales won gold in the 100-meter butterfly.

A lot led up to Rowdy's public display of emotion. For starters, Pablo's mother had just passed away the previous year. Pablo was on Rowdy's original Olympic team in 1984, managing to win relay gold and two silver medals swimming butterfly. He set relay records with teammates Rick Carey, Steve Lundquist, and Rowdy. He tried out again in 1988, but didn't quite manage to make it past trials. In 1992, however, he didn't just return to swim in the Olympics, but he went on to win gold, becoming the oldest swimmer to do so that year. It was his first time to win an individual gold medal. He was 28.

"When he won, it was sort of like seeing myself win the race," Rowdy says, noting the tears shed were tears of sheer joy. "There was a personal connection there for me. Pablo's probably the nicest male swimmer I've ever met."

It wasn't the last time he cried. At those same games, tears fell for his friend Summer Sanders, who won the 200-meter butterfly. And four years later, he struggled to contain his emotions when his close friend, Jeff Rouse, won the 100-meter backstroke in Atlanta.

Shedding tears doesn't always come so easy, not for Rowdy, but he's quick to admit it happens when you're closely connected to someone. These were friends of his, people he knew well. He knew how they were inside and outside the pool.

"They're great swimmers, but even better people," he says. "Summer and Jeff are really good people who deserved to win. When you meet people like that, you can't help but get attached."

One time he didn't cry – but could have, and for altogether different reasons – was when he got passed over to broadcast in 1992. Newcomers Mike O'Brien and Mary Wayte were chosen instead. Each were Olympic medalists who had won in 1984 but, unlike Rowdy, neither had any broadcasting experience.

And that's a little bit like being thrown to the wolves, as Rowdy puts it. It's not backbreaking work by any means. But eighteen-hour days for eight straight days isn't easy to manage either. Nothing truly prepares commentators for what happens when broadcasting for the Games.

"I don't think it worked out for them. From a critical standpoint, the reviews just weren't very good," Rowdy says. "They weren't asked back. It was like they'd been picked off the street. They weren't prepared for all they had to do. And for that kind of a thing, you have to have experience in it."

"Honestly it's really unfair they were put in that kind of a position."

What looks like two talking heads on television, two friends having some casual conversation over the events at play, really amounts to much more. While commentators are chatting with the other commentators on the set, earbuds are piping in directions, suggestions, and facts from producers and directors. And, to make matters that much more stressful, the now-retired president of NBC Sports (Dick Ebersol) would also chime in and offer the occasional comment or two. And it all happens at the same time.

"I mean, they used twenty-eight TV cameras in Beijing," he says. "We had to know every single camera angle."

Learning to navigate that kind of madness was something Rowdy had to teach himself to do, but not without leaning on others for help.

One person even more important to him than his on-air partner and absolutely critical to all he does is Mike Unger. He's the one constantly feeding him information during broadcasts, picking up on all Rowdy might miss. He's in the production truck the entire time and helping produce the show — sort of the man behind the curtain—but his presence is palpable. Mike knows more about swimming than any person he's ever met, Rowdy says.

All things considered, 1992 was a good year. It's an Olympics Rowdy looks back on with a good dose of pride, especially considering it helped set the stage for all that would follow. Since then, he's called every single major swim race.

1996 — Atlanta

For all Rowdy was able to learn in Barcelona, it wasn't until Atlanta that he became an official broadcast analyst for NBC. And, before that could happen, there were tryouts.

Rowdy had to audition. It meant going into a studio with sportscaster Greg Gumbel and talking about a race. He didn't know what race before he arrived, but he had to talk about it all the same, with zero preparation. The next day, they called him up and asked if he'd like to call (or commentate) the Olympics with Dan Hicks, someone he didn't know at the time. The answer was an easy yes.

Now, having sat behind a microphone with Dan Hicks for as long as he has, the two have become close friends, as well as broadcasting partners. He's quick to call two individuals mentors of his; John Naber is one and Hicks is the other.

Not only was Naber a five-time Olympic medalist, he was the first person Rowdy ever worked with on broadcast television. He was the play-by-play guy and had been managing that spot for a decade. As such, he helped Rowdy get comfortable in front of the camera, helping with all the terms and procedures he didn't yet understand.

Hicks picked up where Naber had left off, bringing Rowdy to that next level of expertise. Together, they have helped bring the Olympics into hundreds of millions of homes.

If it weren't for these two men, Rowdy wouldn't be a broadcaster.

"The Atlanta Olympics was awesome in one respect, like the fact that we were doing it live. I love calling races live," Rowdy says. "It's like anchoring a relay (or being the last one to swim on the relay team). I like that pressure. I like having it all on the line and, in the end, there being no room for error. If you make a mistake, there's no way to clean it up."

There's talking about a race as it's happening and there's doing take after take to get it perfect if it's being taped. Set side-by-side, it's easy to see why he prefers the former to the latter.

Consider that two of the Games Rowdy has done have been live and four have been taped. When it's been live, it's been a thrill ride. Rowdy has loved every minute.

Atlanta was an experience better left forgotten. It was his least favorite Olympics. It was the fifth American city to host the Games and the third to host Summer Games. It will also unfortunately be remembered by some for the Centennial Olympic Park bombing that killed one spectator and wounded over a hundred others.

"From a historic standpoint, it didn't have a lot of history, not worldwide," he has said. "It didn't feel like it had that Olympic spirit about it. The organizers did great and seeing Muhammad Ali light the torch was amazing, but I never got into the Olympic spirit there."

2000 — Sydney

The games "down under" in Sydney, Australia helped restore some of the historic tradition that seemed to be missing in Atlanta. But the event was taped and, for Rowdy, that meant enduring longer hours than if it had been a live broadcast event.

He was at the pool twenty hours a day. He was there so much, a mattress was moved into the editing room. It was less than ideal, but it helped cut out any kind of a commute between his long days. It assured he would enjoy at least a solid four hours of rest a night.

Rowdy's wife, Judy, is quick to share that, when Rowdy does a taped Olympics, it takes so much out of him that he sleeps for two solid days afterward; such is his level of physical exhaustion.

It was the Sydney Games that featured Eric Moussambani.

From Equatorial Guinea and known for practicing regularly in a hotel pool leading up to the Games, he wasn't the strongest swimmer there ever was. Still, when two others false-started, they were automatically disqualified, and he was the only man left swimming. He was slow and he almost didn't finish the event he raced in. When he finally did, his time was fairly laughable.

Luckily, and for a lot of reasons to his credit, Rowdy sees Moussambani's race a little differently than most.

"It was a controversial thing, but it was beautiful," he says. "It showed that the Olympics really was for everybody. He wasn't a good swimmer, but he just happened to be that country's best swimmer."

Moussambani became the running joke of Sydney, but he also became the spirit of the Olympics, the embodiment of what the Games are truly about.

One of the perks of being someone with the unique privilege to cover the Olympics for decades is that Rowdy is able to spend time with some of the most elite athletes on the planet. This means he's been able to go to their training camps, fully immerse himself in their culture, discover what motivates them, learn their likes and dislikes, research their backgrounds, and so on. He's allowed a richer perspective than most — he gets to see the bigger picture.

For instance, he had the chance to meet up with the United States swim team in 2000 when they were in San Francisco, just before they left for Australia. He ran into Brooke Bennett, first an Olympic champion in 1996 (and many times since). It was just as she was about to get in the water.

"She proceeds to casually ask me if I want to swim with her," Rowdy says. "I jumped at that opportunity!"

She was swimming a main set that was 40 by 100 on a 1:10 interval. Rowdy lasted about six of them with her before he had to stop completely — and just short of throwing up. And Brooke, much to his surprise, went on to do forty long-course meter intervals, averaging about 1:05 for every single one. With that kind of consistency, it's little wonder that she'd once again become the Olympic champion in the 800 Free and also win the 400 that year.

"It gave me some insight into what she was doing when I was in the water with her," he says. "I'll always remember the experience as being representative of just how incredibly hard she trained."

Sydney is one of his favorite Olympic cities, and not just because Rowdy was recognized as some kind of celebrity. Swimming is regarded as the national pastime in Australia: ninety percent of the country lives within ten miles of the ocean. Australians know the sport, highly regard swimmers, and regularly dominate races.

"A lot of people ask me what my favorite Olympics was: Sydney comes close. Swimming was as big there as football is in America. They know the sport so well that the energy for it was constant; I was known wherever I went, but it goes beyond that. The deep appreciation for swimming was key."

2004 — Athens

As broadcasters in Athens, Rowdy and the rest of the crew were specifically advised against disparaging the Greeks in any possible way while in their country. It was only three years after the tragedy of 9/11 and terrorism was still a big worry at the forefront of everyone's minds. Security was heightened and certain liberties from previous Games were outright taken away.

Still, if he'd been given the opportunity to speak freely, he probably wouldn't have been very complimentary. And, despite the fact it was Michael Phelps' coming-out party with six gold medals, Rowdy was fairly miserable.

Temperatures climbed past 100 degrees. The country had run out of money for the Games, too, so races were happening in an outdoor pool. Originally, it was budgeted to happen indoors. When Rowdy and the other announcers weren't on camera, they were being handed them ice towels to put on their heads. Between races, Rowdy even took to hiding between and under desks to escape the unrelenting sun.

"I've never been so hot in my life," the native Floridian said. "I couldn't even see the monitors because of how bright the sun was."

Only five sports have been in every single Olympics since 1896: track and field, gymnastics, cycling, fencing and — that's right — swimming. In the beginning, swimming took place in the chilly Bay of Zea. Today, Olympians enjoy heated pools.

Still, to see Greece at that time was to see a country unprepared. Roads were unpaved. Flowerbeds were being planted just days before the opening ceremonies. Putting the Games on had broken the country. It's a very big reason Greece has financial problems to this day.

"It was literally a joke. The attitude was like 'Oh, we'll be alright. It's Athens.' And that was sad to see."

That said, Rowdy couldn't help but love the people there. Once the Games were over, he found himself shopping and looking to buy a gift for his wife: He ended up more or less trapped in a tiny jewelry store for six hours. There was food and dancing and people treating him like he was a part of their extended family. It was his own personal version of the My Big Fat Greek Wedding movie.

"They didn't call me by my name, either," he says. "Whenever they wanted me, they'd refer to me as, simply, 'Three-Time Gold Medalist.'"

2008 — Beijing (aka The Michael Phelps Olympics)

Beijing was a thrill, to put it lightly. It couldn't have played out any better had Hollywood gotten hold of it. It made a superstar out of a young swimmer and cemented all-new Olympic records for the United States and the sometimes-popular, sometimes-not sport of swimming. With Michael Phelps and swimming taking center stage, these Olympics helped inspire swimmers at all levels, as well as their friends, families, and viewers who never imagined themselves swimming competitively.

The XXIX Olympic Games reignited Rowdy's love of the world's athletic center stage and continue to stoke his enthusiasm for his sport even today.

As far as Games go, Beijing was the exact opposite of Athens; they were the most dramatic Rowdy had ever witnessed. With the unconquerable Phelps at the helm, he had the chance to see a drama unfold over eight nights. The fast-emerging star won eight gold medals, beating Mark Spitz' previous record of seven, barely winning one of them by a hundredth of a second.

The feat was awe inspiring, even for a semi-retired athlete who had defined his life with Olympic gold.

"Do you know how close that is? That's half of a little fingernail! And, yet, it was the difference between gold and silver. Can you imagine if it had been seven gold [medals] and a silver? That just doesn't have the same ring to it."

One race Phelps helped with – the 400 Freestyle relay – Rowdy calls the greatest swim race in Olympic history. Damin Esper, of Bleacher Report, sides with his opinion, labeling it one of the ten most memorable moments in Olympic swimming history, all due to Jason Lezak's Herculean performance.

The French were favored to win and they knew it. They'd outright said they were going to smash the Americans in the race. The swimmer anchoring the relay for the United States was journeyman sprinter Jason Lezak; he was up against the world record holder from France. He'd never been faster than 47.5 seconds. This time around, though, he went 46.0 – a full second-and-a-half faster than he'd ever done. Essentially, it's the fastest relay split in history. He helped beat the French and Phelps was able to continue his quest for eight gold medals.

Rowdy believes that if Phelps hadn't have won after the third day, no one would have watched the swimming races for the rest of the Olympics. It'd have been over for them. Instead, there were eight days, or an average of a gold medal won every single day. Phelps even won the 200-meter butterfly when his goggles had accidentally filled up with water.

"Essentially, he swam blind," Rowdy says, incredulously. "He counted his strokes for the last 50 and he still won."

Rowdy and his crew were going crazy after the 400 Relay, patting backs and slapping high fives. They knew the excitement would captivate a broader viewership. But not everyone was having the best time at the Games. For example, Rowdy's group shared the same compound as those announcing for the divers. Unfortunately for those commentators, they were having a horrible go at the games in Beijing. By the time the event was over, the U.S. team had not won a single medal.

"And about fifty of us were headed back to the compound when one of the editors of diving came out and he says, 'You guys just called the greatest race in Olympic history and I'm back here editing some Chinese swimmer named Long Dong.'"

The first eight days of the Beijing Olympics were not only the most watched Games in history, but the most watched television event in history. Over 200 million people in the United States tuned in for an average of 25 million viewers a night. But because Rowdy was in China, he had not heard about any of that. He and his cohorts were so caught up calling races, they weren't paying attention to what else was happening. They only realized how huge an event it was once they had returned home.

Altogether, Phelps won fourteen golds in 2004 and 2008. Now, whenever Phelps decides to watch one of his winning races, he hears Rowdy and Dan Hicks helping add emotion to what he was probably feeling.

"We will always have that connection," Rowdy says. "He can't watch his races without hearing my voice! It'd be like watching a movie without any sound. You need that sound."

Phelps swam seventeen races in eight days in Beijing. In 1984, Rowdy swam four races in eight days and thought he was going to die. To contrast the two men even further, Phelps swam a total of 3,300 meters altogether, almost two full miles. Rowdy swam 400 meters in the same amount of time.

"He's the greatest swimmer in history, no doubt about it," Rowdy says. "He changed the sport more than any other person or event."

And that's not just hyperbole. That's a statement backed by numbers. For example, normally swimming has a 3 percent increase in its membership every year. When Phelps won, however, that membership increase shot to 17 percent — six times more than average. As far as Rowdy is concerned, there's only one reason for that: His name is Michael Phelps.

"Anybody can sugarcoat it and say differently, but we owe him so much. We owe him a lot."

Rowdy has his own reasons why Phelps has been as successful as he has been. For one, he's got an incredible feel for the water. His ability to grasp with his hands and feet is nearly unfathomable – every moment he's in the water is non-turbulent. It's allowed him to build a reputation of putting fear into other swimmers. When they get on the blocks, they are already defeated. Every time Phelps broke a world record, he was able to add a little more fear to his would-be opponents.

"Suddenly, everybody was swimming for second," Rowdy says.

By his own calculations, Phelps only took a few days off of swimming in eight years (between 2000 and 2008). He didn't experience what it was like to be someone his own age who wasn't actively training.

It's hard to grasp the magnitude of all Phelps did, and the enormous difficulty behind it. When it was all over, Rowdy was on hand as one of the first people to share that with him. He's quick to use words like "unbelievable" and "epic."

"In my book, he's definitely the greatest Olympian in history," Rowdy says, adding, "He's arguably even the greatest athlete in history."

To help add to the excitement of Beijing, Dick Ebersol had made the calculated decision to broadcast the Olympics live in the United States. Ebersol predicted what Phelps had the ability to do and knew it'd likely reflect in the ratings.

"It's because of [Ebersol] that every single night people would stay up until midnight watching," Rowdy says. "People were cursing me out when I got back because they lost so much sleep."

Dick will go down in Rowdy's book as the most amazing television executive in history. On top of helping create Saturday Night Live, he was behind the first-ever Olympic finals that were done in the morning. Doing so allowed everyone in America to watch them live in primetime.

Because of the 12-hour time difference between Beijing and New York, filming at 10 in the morning overseas allowed for them to play out at 10 at night in America.

"There's nothing better than showing a race live. You just can't beat it," Rowdy says.

Rowdy was sent to the proverbial principal's office at least once. At the Olympic trials in Long Beach (2004), Brendan Hansen, a great American breaststroker, had just set a world record. And when he did, Rowdy said that it was so amazing, he got goosebumps while watching it. Even though he spoke the truth, there was some criticism in the press the following day surrounding that comment alone. Dick called Rowdy in and made certain he knew the comment was silly.

"He jokingly told me to stop smoking the weed before I went on air," Rowdy says. "Needless to say, I have never gotten goosebumps again in a race ... or at least none that I've shared with America."

It's telling to note that the office Dick both worked and slept at the office he had set up at the International Broadcasting Center at each Olympiad. They set up a nice bedroom for him and, during the sixteen days of the Games, he was lucky to get a couple hours of shuteye a night. He was a man with a plan, Rowdy says. What you watch on the telecast from that time is testament to Dick's vision.

Some criticism of Dick and NBC surfaced in the past about showing taped coverage during primetime hours instead of showing it live and as it happens. Rowdy considers it unjustified talk.

"The casual Olympic fan is just like the casual TV fan. They sit home every night and watch a couple of hours of TV. Immediate access to content is important, but why would you want to show something live at three in the morning if nobody's actually awake to watch it? The way it was, you could still look up the results and participate watching it that night with your family."

2012 — London

Rowdy's been part of every Olympic Games around the world since 1984. Sydney appreciated swimming the most, Atlanta and Los Angeles were on his own home turf and Beijing had the spectacle of Phelps. But overall? London wins. From good weather to a strong volunteer force to the level of competition to the way Team USA performed, the London Games hit all the marks.

At that time, it was widely believed London would be the last Olympics Michael Phelps would be a part of. If that had actually happened, Rowdy would have been able to say he was part of every major swim meet of Phelps' twelve-year career. In essence, he saw him become the champion he is today.

"And it was special to see him transform from this shy fifteen-year-old in 2000 to an elder spokesperson for our sport in 2012," Rowdy says. "By the time he'd arrived in London, it was clear it wasn't about him winning gold medals, but what was best for the team."

Rowdy's crew even traveled to France to see the team train. They became so close with the swimmers, they felt a real bond. Team

USA appeared to feel the same way: They put Dan Hicks, poolside commentator Andrea Kremer, and Rowdy in their lip sync of Carly Rae Jepsen's "Call Me Maybe" video that surfaced around that time. It has reached over 13 million views on YouTube. (You can spot them dancing in the last thirty seconds.)

The only bad thing he can conjure up when it comes to London is the fact it was a taped Olympics. (Beijing and Atlanta were the only ones to be broadcast live.) Most of the races he was involved in were "live to tape," which meant they would record the race as if it were live, to give it that same feel. But when it came right down to it, people already knew the end result before ever watching the race. They might not have the video available, but the results had showed up earlier in the day.

"Twenty years ago, it wouldn't have been a problem," Rowdy says. "Now I get results sent to my phone instantly via text message."

The difference between a text and video is not only watching the drama unfold; it's also hearing the verbal play-by-play that heightens the unfolding drama in a way a simple recount of the results can never quite match.

The year 2012 was the year of two American women: Katie Ledecky and Missy Franklin. Ledecky was just fifteen years old, someone Rowdy is quick to call "the sweetest girl in the whole world." She won the Women's 800 Freestyle and gave the world a glimpse of how incredible she was. What's more, Nathan Adrian won the 100 Free, the same event Rowdy had won in 1984. It created an instant bond. The United States hadn't won in that event since 1988. When Adrian won, he did so just barely—by a hundredth of a second. Not surprisingly, Rowdy got pretty emotional about it.

Nathan took home two gold medals and a silver, too. And Katie has turned into the most dominating swimmer on the planet. At the 2015 World Championships, she won the 200, 400, 800, and 1500 Freestyle.

"It would be like Carl Lewis winning the 100, 200, 400, and 800 in track and field," Rowdy says. "It was a complete domination of almost all freestyle events."

It was nice to have the Olympics not completely centered on Phelps. Team USA had a lot of individual gold medalists, in fact.

Rowdy remembers the most controversial part of London being that he wouldn't believe Phelps' retirement news, not for a minute. He all but guaranteed he'd be back and said so on air. People got borderline angry, wondering why he couldn't accept Phelps saying what he'd said, but it went far beyond that for Rowdy. At age 27,

Phelps was simply too young to retire. In Rowdy's mind, he still had a lot to give to the sport. And in the end, Rowdy was right. Phelps hopes to keep competing; he will be vying to be part of the team in Rio.

"Once you experience the Olympics – and especially once you win – it's intoxicating, that feeling. It's hard to walk away from that, I don't care who you are."

2016 – Rio

One of the reasons Rowdy so looks forward to Rio in 2016? It'll be live again, which translates to nobody knowing race results before they actually take place. They'll be broadcast on primetime television no less. Swimming will take place live in Rio from 10 p.m. to midnight (or 9 p.m. to 11 p.m. Eastern time) meaning more eyes will see the events unfold live, all over the world. Another reason to celebrate ahead of time: It's the first time the Games have been to South America in their 116-year history. That's fairly amazing in and of itself, regardless of some opposition to the Games heading to those shores.

Based on his unique relationship with the Olympics over three decades, Rowdy is optimistic.

"Some naysayers are saying [Brazil] won't be prepared, that the water is polluted and the country is running out of money but, you know what? They say those kinds of things every four years. And every single Olympics turns out okay."

When Rowdy and Dan Hicks take their places in Rio, it will be a momentous occasion all its own. It will mark their seventh Olympic Games together, which adds up to twenty years of delivering the Olympic story to a world stage. Not only that, but they will be the longest running commentating duo in history for a single sport.

On his own, Rowdy has commentated for thirty years. Starting in 1985, and in addition to his six Olympics, he's also called six world championships, twenty five men's NCAA championships and twenty one women's NCAA championships.

"I can't begin to tell you how blessed I am," Rowdy says, noting he'll be a fifty-seven-year-old in Rio. "I'm not that religious, but if there is a God, he's shined down on me."

As for what the future holds beyond Rio and into the 2020 Games, Rowdy has his immediate doubts. Would he love to continue to be attached to the sport? That's an easy yes. But, he says, he'll be sixty one years old. His future is uncertain in a medium dependent on drawing new, young audiences.

Top five Olympic moments

5. Misty Hyman. She won gold in the 200m Butterfly in Sydney (2000). What made that special to me was the fact she was swimming against the most popular female athlete in the country (Susan O'Neil, otherwise known as Madame Butterfly), who was a huge favorite. O'Neil had already won gold at this point and Misty was practically a nobody. Nobody gave her a chance, she was a huge underdog, and she'd been coached by my late coach, Richard Quick. So I had a bit of a personal connection through him. He told me a week before the Games that she would win the gold, but her time had been coming in at four seconds slower. I laughed … but, in the end, she did. She really did. She went really fast, hung on and won the gold medal. At the time, I was quick to call it the greatest upset in swimming Olympic history. When we turned it over to Bob Costas, he said I could think of a bigger upset than that and started talking hockey teams, but I corrected him before he could get too far down that road: "I said Olympic swimming history, not Olympic history, Bob." Misty beat Susan in her home country, was not favored to even make the finals and she's really a very, very sweet girl.

4. 800 Freestyle Relay in Athens, Greece (Men's). It was so cool because the Americans were huge underdogs and Australia anchored with a guy named Ian Thorpe. Klete Keller anchored for America and he won it for them. It was a cool moment because, well, I always love an underdog, whether it's the U.S. or another country. And I love relays. Up to that point, it was the greatest Olympic relay I had ever seen. I see myself in the underdog role a little bit, especially because I'd started so late; on my way up, I was always the underdog. I tend to like that feeling. I always like being the chaser and not the chased. That alone kept me humble and kept me hungry. Most of the underdogs that have come out on top have an innocence about them, a naiveté that the world doesn't revolve around them. More times than most, nobody even knows who they are. And that was the case with Klete Keller.

3. Pablo Morales (1992). I've made mention of this one before, but the story goes that his father had just died and he truly was the nicest male swimmer I've ever met in my life. We won a gold medal together in '84. We swam in a relay together. And, even though he was favored hugely for the '88 Games, he didn't make the team. Four years later, he comes back and, this time, guess what? Yes, he's the underdog, completely past his prime. I can relate to him because of my own situation in '84. To this day, I say he looked up at me and raised his finger, pointing right at me after he'd won. It's like when Michael Jordan waved at me at a Bulls game and nobody sitting around me believed it to be true, but it's what happened. It's what really happened.

2. Michael Phelps winning the 100 Fly by 1/100th of a second. His is the only non-underdog moment on my list. It's the race that defined Michael Phelps' perfect storm of 2008. This race was going to be the toughest for Michael on paper. A guy named Michael Cavic was his only equal and this was Phelp's shortest race, one that he was going to be definitely vulnerable. Cavic had more speed than anyone on the planet in his first 50. The problem for him was his last 25. This would be Phelps' seventh gold medal matching Mark Spitz and we knew it was going to be a huge television moment. And it was déjà vu all over again as Cavic was about a body length ahead but Dan I were careful not to say it was the end as we both knew he had amazing closing speed. Phelps chased him down and won the gold medal by 1/100th of a second! Dan was going crazy, I was going crazy and I knew America would be going crazy. My dad later told me I sounded like a little girl when he heard my high-pitched voice that night.

1. The Men's 400 Freestyle Relay in Beijing (2008), when Michael Phelps was right in the middle of winning his eight gold medals. The Americans were considered huge underdogs and were told repeatedly that they were going to get smashed like a guitar. What's funny is Gary Hall had said the same thing to the Australians in 2000 and we ended up getting beat then. This time, though? Jason Lezak came in at the end and won it. That race, specifically, that one was a turning point for Phelps and America and all that happened after it.

Nature, Nurture

Much has been written about what makes a champion. Why someone evolves into an inspiration isn't necessarily easy to decipher. Some would look to parents and try to figure out how he or she was raised. Others might chalk things up to a relentless coach. If it was as easy as plugging in some kind of winning formula, our world would be a far different one than it is today.

When considering Rowdy Gaines, the champion's drive, motivation, and determination are likely rooted in his upbringing.

His dad, Buddy, talks about how he was a gypsy dad during the '60s. He liked to film and direct movies and commercials and even got to photograph Frank Sinatra once. He'd spend six months of the year in Chicago and the other six in Los Angeles. A few hours with him may lead to stories of past celebrities and forgotten names of those he came across on a regular basis. He might even bring up how he shot an entire motion-picture-length film underwater (aptly, if not emphatically, titled *Scuba!*), a film considered the *Endless Summer* of movies for scuba divers.

When it comes to his ideas about raising his two children, Buddy said he worked to instill in them the belief that they were anything but average. Whatever they tried, he knew they would devote themselves and stand out from the crowd. Whatever it was they did, no matter what it was they chose to go into or try their hand at, he believed they'd do that thing, those things, whatever they were, and they would do them rather well.

Buddy got his wish. He'll be the first to tell you that his son was fortunate to have the skills, abilities and drive to prevail at most things in high school, whether it meant high marks on his tests or fastest lap times in the pool: Rowdy didn't want to be third in the top three. He cared little about coming in second place. He wanted to be the best, the very best.

"That was his way," Buddy says. "Rowdy is not normal or average. He's a real wimp at home and a nice enough guy in the office, but he's a gorilla in the pool."

And that's an image to mull over – a gorilla in the pool. If Rowdy has practiced in a hotel pool some early morning, it's easy to discover he's been there: Some might argue more water ends up out of it than in it after just an hour of swimming. And it's loud. He probably wakes more than a few of his sleepy traveling neighbors in the process. In the pool, he is king. It's the space he knows; it's his domain. Take that into consideration and the comparison to a gorilla gets a whole lot clearer.

There's a lesson to be taken from the way Rowdy swims, too, according to Buddy. It is inseparably attached to his becoming an Olympian. Both of Buddy's children swim – daughter Tracy got a scholarship in swimming and still swims today – but there was something that made his son very different from his daughter. While she was as good a swimmer as he was when racing, Rowdy wouldn't let a single person in front of him. Not just sometimes, either.

"Ever."

"Even though Tracy was fast, people got in front of her," Buddy says. "I have watched him swim for years and years and years and I've never seen anybody get in front of him, not once. If it ever happened, I never saw it."

The sun is setting on his island home in Little Gasparilla, but he has more to say. Catching the last light of day with his eyes, they sparkle a bit as he continues.

"One of my most thrilling moments as a father is when he said, 'Dad, I am going to try to break 20 seconds.' So he swam in a real fast pool in Ohio and he did it, just like that. And, I'm telling you, I was as impressed by that as his winning a gold medal. That was huge! It would be like a runner doing a four-minute mile."

There's a difference between a father who is proud of his son and a son who deserves to be bragged about. Rowdy's tendency toward routine and drive became evident to other members of his family early on. Speaking on the telephone from her hometown in Winter Haven, his sister shared how Rowdy's talent is something that would be flat out hard to duplicate.

"A parent can't make his or her child be a certain way. I just think it's innate," Tracy says. "I don't know why he was the way he was. Nothing was forced on him. He had the talent. Within a month of his swimming for the high school team, you could tell he had a gift. People don't jump to the level he did after a month."

To add to that, there was a fair amount of self-discipline to attach to that competitive spirit that never really lagged, not as far as she could tell. Once Rowdy finally understood where it was he wanted to go with swimming, he didn't deter from his vision.

Tracy recalled how he needed structure to propel himself

forward as well.

"Even when he was five or six years old, he would say, 'Tracy, I have to go to bed now. I'm tired, so we have to go to bed.' And I'd be lying there with my eyes wide open. Everything was routine for him." As for the competition? Her older brother would not let her win, whether it was the two of them swimming or something altogether different.

"We'd be driving to Mississippi to see our grandparents, for example, and we'd fight about who would cross the state line before the other one did, to the point of him jumping over me and into the front seat of the car so he'd get there first. That's the monster I had to live with."

Still, when it came to his being a swimmer, to honing all his ability to make something of it, Tracy can't help but recognize that he fought to get there. Nothing was handed to him.

"I remember visiting Rowdy when he was staying with Billy Forester [an Olympian from 1976] and they lived in a filthy, nasty neighborhood in a shack with no furniture and just a couple of mattresses. That's how he lived; it was all about swimming. Nothing else mattered."

Even though that was the case, it wasn't always his ability to swim that people were wont to recognize in the man. His strong family background helped him build a character that often made lasting impressions.

"He's simply one of the most honest and sincerest people I've ever met in my life," says Dick Carson, owner of the Las Vegas Gold swim team that Rowdy once coached. "I've met a few like that in my time, but there are not many I can say that about without any doubt and hesitation. He's one of them."

It's for that reason alone that, when he learned of Rowdy's being hospitalized in 1992, Dick didn't take any time to question the specifics. He was on a plane to Hawaii to help his friend out for the weeks it'd take for him to get better, sitting with him for hours on end and even helping him take his first steps after being paralyzed.

Judy says that, every single time Dick came around, Rowdy's vital signs would improve. But Dick says he was just there to support a close friend.

"A lot of times Rowdy could have taken advantage of me or told me a lie and could have done things that wouldn't have been all that bad in the end, but he didn't. He chose not to."

Such insights about his character underscore that, in an era when sports heroes are often defined by ego-driven excesses, Rowdy stands out as a champion who has managed to embrace humility and stay rooted in his family and friends.

Rowdy's take

There are many words or directives that go into becoming an Olympic champion. I was never perfect by any stretch of the imagination, but I tried to live by these, and I did so consistently. Did I mess up? Absolutely. But I was always living by this code, by the value of these words.

If I made mistakes, which I did, it was always good because I learned from them. When I failed to live up to these things (again, which I did, repeatedly), I learned from the experience. I rarely made the same mistake twice. That's why I was successful in the pool. That consistency paid off.

Swimming is not for the faint of heart. In my opinion, it is the most difficult sport in the world to train for. So if you make those mistakes, it's a lot harder to make them again. You don't want to make them again.

The first word I live by – that I have always lived by – is dedication. As general as that is, it applies to the fact that swimming is such a demanding sport. We don't have any other choice but to be dedicated. If I wanted to be a soccer player, I could work out once or twice a week. But what about 10 miles a day of swimming? Try and imagine that! To me, it demands dedication through good times or bad. Our lives are full of peaks and valleys. We ride this roller coaster through life. To me, the real champions live through the good (or easy), but also live successfully through the tough (or bad) times. It's those tough times that help define who you are.

When I went to practice the first day in the morning, the pool to me was so easy. It felt like it was a foot deep, every stroke came easily and that first 1,000 yards was a piece of cake. But, once I got to the 15,000-yard mark, it got a lot harder. Beginning to end, you have to be focused on the task at hand. For me, that dedication and commitment were for one reason and one reason alone: It was all about going to the Olympics. That's the rabbit that was always in front of me. I was the greyhound chasing the rabbit around the track over and over again. I was that stupid dog, you know? I had to block out that 10 miles a day, thinking of that and that alone, or I would have quit.

I've got a personal story that illustrates my point.

When you race, your swimsuit is very tight. I used to wear a size thirty-inch waist once upon a time, but, when I raced, I'd wear a suit with twenty-four-inch waist. In 1979, I had swum at an event earlier in the meet in Los Angeles at our National Championships and, after the race, I just had to get out of it. It was squeezing my "fatherly love" way too tight. It was killing me! You can't wear it for long. So, I took it off, put on sweats, didn't bother with putting on any underwear and I continued on with the day.

At my next race, just an hour later, I'd forgotten I'd taken my suit off. I walked out on deck and started talking to my coach. He was telling me how he wanted me to swim the race and giving me strategy and stuff and, in the course of all that, he said he wanted me to get back in the pool and start warming up. So I took my sweats off and, still standing there in a T-shirt, I handed my sweats to my coach and started to stretch. And it got kind of quiet. There were a thousand people gathered there to watch and somebody yells from the stands, "Rowdy, look down." Keep in mind that, all the while, the greatest female swimmer in history was sitting next to me, Tracy Caulkins.

So I did it. I looked ... and, of course, I was completely naked from the waist down! I fell to the ground, sat down, covered myself up as best I could and yelled at my coach to give me a towel. He hadn't noticed, either. And Tracy leans over and says, "Rowdy, it's not that big of a deal." I said, "Ha, ha … very funny."

She went on to break a world record and I'm the one who should get credit for it! And 20 minutes later, I swam my race, won a national title and broke a world record, all at once. So, through the good times and bad, you should never lose your focus. You should always, always stay dedicated to the task at hand.

Second, don't be afraid to fail. I had a coach who was never afraid to take risks. He wasn't afraid to fail. For example, in 1982, our sport went to a no-false-start rule. And, before that year, you were allowed to false-start, which would allow you to get off the blocks quicker and end up with a faster time. The starter could say 'Take your mark" and you could dive in and not get disqualified. You could do it a second time. But, the third time, you'd be disqualified individually. And, before then, every single person put both feet forward on the blocks when the starter said 'Swimmers, take your mark." They would step up, put their toes around the blocks, grab the block and go forward. When I'd do a regular grab start, I'd grab both feet and I'd lean in and false start. I'd fall in the pool, no matter what. When they went to the no false start rule, I didn't know what I was going to do. So

I put one foot forward, one back and that gave me some stability on the blocks. I'd use my arms and back foot to do my start. And nobody had ever done it that way before.

Dara Torres and I were the first ones to use the track start in any competition. Dara was a sensational young sprinter, tall and lengthy. She had the same problem I did with the grab start. So her coach got us together and we brainstormed on how we could get down and off the blocks quicker. I think we were inspired by the track and field athletes, especially in the 100-meter dash. When Dara and I went to a meet in Europe in the winter of 1982, we decided to test it over there.

We were the first ones to use it, too, because we were the first ones to get disqualified for doing it. After we did our races in Paris and won, we each got out of the water, only to get immediately disqualified by the referee. He said that what we had done was against the rules, but only because no one had ever done it before. They checked and discovered there really was nothing in the rulebook against it and we later got reinstated. Dara, Dara's coach, and I were pioneers of that move.

And, at forty-eight years old, she's still using it and is still a world-class swimmer. Now every swimmer uses it. They even call it the "Gaines" start in Japan. But, in the 1984 Olympics, only two people used it, Mary T. Meagher (who won three gold medals) and me.

The moral of the story is I was not afraid to take that risk and fail. I failed miserably in that start. Three months later, I did that track start at the world championships in 1982 in Ecuador. I got to the finals and my back foot slipped off the back of the blocks and I did a belly flop in the water. I came in eighth place but, unfortunately, there were only eight swimmers, so I was dead last. I vowed never to make that mistake again. And, for the next two years, I told myself I'd be the last swimmer out of the water every single practice. I worked my start. I wanted to get it right. So I'd do two or three more runs than everyone else would. And, at the Olympics, I was off the blocks the quickest. I practiced that start and it paid off.

Third, be a leader, not a follower. Be original in your thinking. Have originality. In my sport, just like in business, there are certain trends you have to follow. The ones that are the best are the ones that are original in their thinking. Apple doesn't really care what anyone else is doing. They don't even go to CES [Consumer Electronics Show]. They don't go! They have their own. They are not followers. And that was my mentality when I stepped in the pool every day. I wanted to lead the lane. There were three to five swimmers in every lane, but I always wanted to lead the lane. I wanted to be first because the guy out front is working the hardest; there was no such thing as catching the draft. In the end, I knew it was better for me. I never ever swam unless I tried to lead the lane. I knew the payoff would still be there in the end.

Another example of a great leader is David Berkoff, a fantastic backstroker. In 1988, he was not very fast at the backstroke when he was on the top of the water, but very, very good at doing the dolphin kick when he was underneath the water. When he got to the Games, he swam 75 percent of that race underwater! The result? He went in there and won a gold and also a silver medal. What he did became known as The Berkoff Blastoff. He was not afraid to be a leader.

Fourth, if you're to approach perfection, it takes a fair amount of repetition. Repetition, repetition, repetition. Practice makes perfect. You have to do it over and over again. There's unfortunately no pixie dust I can sprinkle on swimmers to make it happen for them. Swimming can be a very boring and monotonous sport. It's doing things over and over again until you get them right.

I used to do some work with a company and they taught that, if you place a high enough value on something, you will figure out how to accomplish that task regardless of how difficult it is. Think about how valuable it is to you, whatever it is.

Consider it this way. Think of having a child who is five years of age or younger (and, if you're a mother or a father, that child is your own). Now, visualize you're on one end of the pool and on the other there is a $100 bill. Would you swim over there? Sure you would! Now you're on the end of a pool that you can't see the other end of. I have the power to create huge 10-foot swells. I have the power to dump sharks in the pool. Great whites, hammerheads, the biggest man-eaters on earth. You're on one end of the pool and I'm on the other: Would you swim now? For a million dollars, you probably wouldn't do it. And, all of a sudden, I have that five-year-old child of yours and I've got him or her on the other side of the pool. I will drop that child in the pool if you don't swim. Would you do it then? A parent would do it in a heartbeat. If you are a mom or a dad, it's hard not to be in tears just thinking about that.

The point is, all of a sudden, it becomes valuable to them. If only one thing meant something to them, it's their child. If there is a high enough value placed on something, you find a way to do it. My child, so to speak, was the Olympics. That's where I had placed my value. That's why my pool was 25 yards long and, by the end of the day, I couldn't see the end of it. And I was swimming with sharks. I approached perfection for that reason alone.

Fifth and finally, never underestimate the value of teamwork. I wish I could have won 40 gold medals so I could give one to each of my 1984 teammates. I felt the energy and power behind every one of them. I know I couldn't have done it without them behind me. I believe in karma. I felt the energy of the crowd. I had to whenever I swam. And, nearly every time I did, I used my team. I always felt like the power of more is better than the power of one. I really felt my teammates cheering for me. Whether they actually meant it or not, I could hear it and feel it. It was one of the big reasons for my success. It's virtually impossible for you to do anything by yourself and succeed. To have the weight of the world on your shoulders is a recipe for disaster. When you feel like an island, it sucks. If you feel like you're by yourself, it sucks. It doesn't work. And that includes training. It's why I hate swimming by myself. You want to feel like other people are struggling along with you and in pain too.

At the Olympics, it's cool because all the different people from different countries are staying in this one unique village. There are 10,000 athletes all in one village. And, in '84, it was at the campus of the University of Southern California. Can you imagine the cafeteria in that village, feeding all the athletes from over the world?

John Naber, a great Olympic champion (and someone I've mentioned before), tells a story that I believe is a great example of teamwork, but in a little bit of a different way.

One morning, he decided to get an early start. So it was four o'clock in the morning and there was just one other guy in the cafeteria and he didn't even look like an athlete. His warmups were all torn up and he wasn't really built very well. And he decided to sit with him. He didn't speak English and they kind of nodded to one another and he takes a tea bag and he breaks it open and pours it into his cup, then pours hot water over it. And John is thinking to himself ... this guy doesn't know the tea bag paper is okay. He doesn't know what you're supposed to do with it. So John takes a tea bag and says, "Excuse me ... paper okay. Paper okay." The other athlete is looking at him like he was strange until he puts the teabag in and the brown starts coming out of the bag. His eyes got real wide and he was sincerely amazed! He slapped his forehead. He couldn't believe it.

And John thought, well, isn't this wonderful? Here he was, teaching culture to this guy from Outer Mongolia. And, the next thing this guy did was take a packet of sugar, he throws it in the tea and starts stirring it and goes "Paper okay. Paper okay." The moral is teamwork, yes. You always want to help a brother out. It's just that, sometimes, it doesn't always work. The last thing John said before walking away was, "Yeah, go ahead and drink it. Paper okay."

Lifesaver

Now in his mid-fifties, Rowdy won his gold medals over three decades ago. And yet, he chooses to keep that proverbial torch lit. He even has a swimsuit sponsor with Arena, one of the biggest swimwear companies in the world. While some former Olympians have gone from gaining their lofty accolades to shifting elsewhere – becoming everything from successful businessmen to moving as far as they could possibly get from the water – he's chosen to keep going and in an altogether different kind of way. He's remained on as role model who champions the sport he holds so dear while reaching beyond, too, toward an even broader audience.

Looking around his office at the YMCA, you're bombarded by reminders of a glorious time gone by. It's a pretty fantastic one-man exhibit ,too.

There he is, shaking hands with George Bush Sr., or Jimmy

Carter or Ronald Reagan. And there's that jumping shirtless spandex shot of him they used in an American Express ad (along with one-time teammate Steve Lundquist), shot by the great Annie Leibovitz, no less. There's a framed photograph of a baby swimming underwater, his father nearby, arms wide and ready to assist. And if you snoop around enough, you'll even find the aforementioned dusty photograph on his desk of an 80s-era superstar, his arm thrown around rock and roll legend Joan Jett.

If you didn't happen to know who Rowdy was in 1984, the photos and awards adorning these walls tell their own stories. For the ones that need explaining or elaborating, he's a treasure trove of facts, a long list of tales and remembrances leading up to — and including — his present day.

There are ready indications he isn't the U.S. poster boy he once was. He's the first to lament he doesn't have all the hair he once did. It's apparent he's acquired more lines on his face (some laugh, some worry). That, and he still feels repercussions from the Guillain-Barre Syndrome that paralyzed him: he still can't entirely feel the tips of his fingers. A history of ear infections has even wreaked some havoc on his ability to hear everything the first time it's said. And it's not uncommon for him to be warming himself next to a space heater in the midst of a hot Florida summer's day.

But that smile seen atop a podium once upon a time? That winning attitude that helped define a triumphant America when it needed a shot of optimism? Both are still there; neither shows any sign of going away.

The tolls of age notwithstanding, so many tidbits about the Olympian remain largely the same. At a relatively young-looking fifty seven years of age, Rowdy still spends his lunch hour in the pool swimming. He still competes in Masters tournaments whenever and wherever he can, as far away as Japan or China or more nearby Arizona or Orlando.

And so the man whose life has ended up shaped by swimming continues to swim, far past the point he ever honestly thought he would.

"It helps me," he admits. "I'm a better person when I swim."

His wife will attest to that, as will his father or really anyone else who has been around Rowdy when a misstep of a schedule has kept him out of the pool for 24 hours or so. In fact, the second he gets out of the pool, he starts thinking about when he'll be able swim next. Such is his ritual and desire to do more, swim more, be more.

You see that in his satisfied face, when he returns from the pool, the hair on his head still poking up from the back. He doesn't care to shower after his swimming workout as he's grown fond of the way chlorine smells. And just because he'll readily apologize later for "that smell" when folks near him pick up on his secret, he'll continue to treat it like it's his own personal cologne. It's a habit created a long time ago, one that has stuck. It will continue to be part of his character, along with the other habits he'd collected along the way. He's one of those habit hoarders.

In his office, Rowdy keeps a red Betta fish on his desk. He never owns up to a reason for getting the fish in the first place and, though many of his fish-related conversations end abruptly in, "Oh, it's just a fish," you quickly pick up that he has some kind of kinship with the animal.

"I have actual dreams at night about being a fish, where I swim with the dolphins and am able to live underwater, moving at their same speed," he says, impossibly excited. "I've had them all my life, for about as long as I can remember."

"It makes sense. I'm more comfortable in the water than I am on land."

The one continuing theme of his dreams, aside from the fact they always deal with some body of water and swimming, is that he is able to breathe underwater. Think Kevin Costner in that colossal bomb of a movie *Waterworld* and you've a peek into a kind of existence he says he'd like to be a part of one day.

"If you think about something so much, it's only natural that you end up dreaming about it. It's really simple. I love the water. I dream about being in it when I'm not."

As for the dream he still holds to when he's awake, there are some ready similarities there too. Think of them as an extension of all he's involved himself with throughout the course of his life.

A long-time advocate for children's safety, Rowdy very much wants to open a swim school one day, one that bears his name. There's an abandoned swimming pool not far from where he lives in Lake Mary, Florida. He'd like to transform it into a place where he teaches children to swim. He envisions it will be a family establishment: One of his daughters will run a café, cooking various culinary delights while two others will help teach swimming lessons, alongside their dad. It would allow those visiting to learn to keep their heads above the water; it would teach them survival.

That said, he's doing more than just dream of it happening. As the vice president of Aquatics for the YMCA of Central Florida where he works full time, he currently oversees twenty-eight pools on a daily basis.

"All I care about is teaching kids how they can be as safe as they can be in the water," Rowdy says.

With so many children dying in what is the second leading cause of death among those aged eight to fourteen (auto accidents is first), he'd like nothing more than to be a part of the solution to that sad statistic. It's something he talks about a lot.

"It drives me crazy to hear about kids who drown. Water safety is huge for me. It's dear to my heart."

It's a big reason why he's so passionate about the YMCA and the USA Swimming Foundation. The organizations help provide scholarships and offer swimming lessons to children of families who could not otherwise afford them.

"Drowning is a silent killer," he says. "It's not like the movies, where you hear them scream as it's taking place. In fact, 60 percent of all children who drown do so when they're within 100 yards of an adult. Half of them happen while the adult is actually watching them."

"I want to really be a part of the solution. Fortunately, there is a cure for most drownings. It comes down to two simple words: swim lessons."

The swim school is a possibility he can actually see happening, provided he takes the necessary steps to get there. He just needs to come up with an estimated three-quarters of a million dollars in funding.

"It's a pipe dream, I know that," he says with a sigh. "But it's a good one. What could be better than teaching kids how to swim?"

Not only are the numbers staggering, but certain populations are more vulnerable than others, as these findings show:

- Each day, ten people drown in the United States.
- Seventy percent of African American children and 60 percent of Hispanic children are unable to swim.
- Fatal, unintentional drowning rates for five-year-old to fourteen-year-old African American children are more than three times higher than their Caucasian counterparts.

The USA Swimming Foundation is working hard to change these statistics. They believe swimming lessons can reduce childhood drownings by 88 percent.

Rowdy worked for the USA Swimming Foundation for five years (2003-2008) and is still an ambassador. The foundation has nearly 800 partners across the United States teaching children the lifesaving skill of learning to swim. All monies raised have provided more than 70,000 scholarships to provide swim lessons to kids who might not otherwise have had the opportunity. Over the past eight years, local partners have reached more than four million kids. Rowdy is quick to say the group is "truly saving lives."

Still, accidents do happen, and they're unfortunately frequent. Sometimes they hit even closer to home than he'd like them to. Not very many years ago, Rowdy was set to open the aforementioned swim school he's dreamed of. When it came right down to it, however, he wasn't able to. The timing was off and wouldn't quite work; he was unable to take that much-required leap of faith. Three months after making that decision, a two-year-old girl drowned in her backyard pool. She lived just a few blocks from where the school would have existed. Try as he might, Rowdy couldn't help but be heartbroken once he learned the news.

"I had a tremendous amount of guilt about that, thinking maybe she'd have been able to take lessons at my school had we opened it," he says. That said, he knows his involvement with the YMCA is allowing him to help on a broader scale than he had ever imagined.

"Drowning doesn't have to take place. Every parent should

teach their child how to be safe in the water. Swim lessons can take down the risk by ninety percent. And if I have to talk to people about this for the rest of my life to get them to understand that, I will."

In addition to dedicating himself to a group that prioritizes swim safety, he also commits himself to a group best known for training elite swimmers. The USA Swimming Foundation is committed to building champions – in the pool and in life. The group was on track in 2016 to provide more than $600,000 to support the U.S. National Team. They plan to offer that same level of financial support in 2016. Rowdy, who moonlighted as a hotel desk clerk and lived in virtual squalor during his Olympic training days, said that kind of money could have made a difference for him. And it actually does make a difference for today's athletes, he added; none of them ever earned what someone like Michael Phelps does today.

"They do this as a job and barely get by. So this money helps as much today as it would have helped me in 1984," the Olympian said.

If Rowdy Gaines had received that kind of assistance during his formative years, one wonders if he'd have become the driving force the swimming world is now so familiar with. He became the person he is on account of his perseverance and desire, someone more keen on creating solutions than viewing setbacks as roadblocks. Because he committed, he repeatedly won. And because he won, he made a habit of doing so, of prevailing and thriving.

He refuses to give up, no matter what area of his life it involves. When faced with an Olympic boycott, he continued to swim, right up until he was actually able to compete and win. When he contracted Guillain-Barre Syndrome and was paralyzed from the neck down, he defeated it, teaching himself to both swim and win again. And when he started on as an Olympic broadcaster, rising to become one of the voices most often heard during the Games, he's not stopped in twenty years. Seeing and hearing him connected to those races is like returning to see and hear an old friend every four years.

There's a reason his many sponsors, contracts and associations stretch so far and include: Liberty Mutual, The Limu Company, Arena Swimwear, Yamamoto Kogaku of Japan, Endless Pools, USA Swimming Foundation, ZAC Foundation, Asphalt Green NY, NBC, ESPN, Swim Across America, Big 10 Network, Pac 12 Network, SEC Network and YMCA of Central Florida.

Rowdy Gaines is the kind of champion few ever have the chance to associate with in their lifetime. His examples of self-sacrifice and commitment are as powerful now as they ever were. His is a story worth learning about, telling and sharing with others. Even better, it's a story that hasn't stopped being told, not yet.

Just as he was doing a quarter century ago in that lifeguard stand, he's as dedicated as he ever has been to the sport of his lifetime. The only thing that's changed is his vantage point. Today, Rowdy is able to connect with millions – from children learning to swim in gator-infested lakes to Olympians trying to make a comeback.

And like the Betta fish he's so fond of, he'll keep right on swimming.

Rowdy's Take

I love lists. And I love swimming. So it's natural for me to want to put together my list of the greatest swimmers in history. These lists are my opinion only and there are arguments for my "honorable mentions" to move up in the ranks. I do not include any of the athletes of the East German Regime because of the systematic doping endeavor that was proven beyond a doubt. I am also reluctant to include any of the Chinese athletes of the early to mid '90s when they had their problems as well.

I base my criteria in each category on the following reasons, in order of importance.

The greatest swimmers in history

1. **Olympic performance, meaning individual gold medals.** Unfortunately, as the old saying goes, "gold is gold and silver is last" and it's so true in our sport. The Olympic gold medal will always be the measuring stick for me to determine if you belong in the top of any of my categories. And it has to be individual gold medals. Relays don't count at least at the top (see number 5). Exceptions: The boycott of the 1980 Olympics is taken into account, as are the cancellation of the 1940 and 1944 Olympics.
2. **World Records**. Even though I would trade a hundred world records for one gold medal as records are and will always be broken, a world record means you are the best swimmer on the planet in that event. That's a pretty good reason to put world records as number two.
3. **Longevity**. I don't like a flash in the pan. It doesn't hold as much weight in your performance in one Olympics or breaking world records in a one or two-year span. The longer you remain on top in the toughest sport in the world, the better. That is incredibly important.
4. **Consistency**. This goes along with longevity but the critical part of this is performing consistently over a long period of time.

5. **Versatility**. This only matters when we talk about the greatest all around swimmers. If you wonder why I might leave someone off who was great in just one stroke, this would be the reason.

6. **Olympic medals (including relays)**. The more medals you have, the better off you are.

I do not put much emphasis on World Championships because they only started in 1975 and it would be unfair to those who did not have a chance to compete in these meets. Also, national titles don't count for much as I am looking at what they do against the world, not what they do against their own country.

The ten greatest male swimmers in history

1. **Michael Phelps**. He is, hands down, the single greatest swimmer in history and it's not even close. Consider his eighteen Olympic gold medals (twenty-two overall and he's not done yet), thirty-nine world records and a career spanning sixteen years at or near the top in so many different events. He is the greatest athlete in history. He changed swimming more dramatically than any person, period.

2. **Mark Spitz**. Pre-Michael, he was the greatest. Nine gold

medals (eleven total) and thirty three world records in five different events. He competed in two Olympic Games and could have done even more, but he retired at the age of twenty two. Even though it was before the so-called Media Age, he put swimming on the map and changed our sport forever.

3. **Johnny Weismuller**. TARZAN! Five gold medals, a bronze in water polo, fifty six national championships, sixty seven world records to his name. And, most importantly, he never lost a race. I repeat, he never lost a race! We will leave out his personal proclivities.

4. **Ian Thorpe**. With five gold medals (nine total), the "Thorpedo" was the youngest world champion at fourteen years of age; he has broken thirteen individual world records during his career.

5. **Ryan Lochte.** Eleven Olympic medals and three Olympic teams. Eighty nine medals in major international competition. If there was no Michael Phelps, he might just have been the greatest.

6. **Matt Biondi**. He almost duplicated Spitz in '88 when he won five golds, one silver and a bronze. With eight gold medals (thirteen total), and seven individual world records in his career, I'm just lucky I got to swim with him at the end of my career and the beginning of his when we won the 400 Free relay in L.A.

7. **Gary Hall Jr.** He carried on his family's legacy by swimming in three Olympic Games and winning ten Olympic medals including back to back 50 freestyles in 2000 and 2004.

8. **Grant Hackett.** The greatest male distance swimmer in history. He won the men's 1500 meters freestyle at both the 2000 Summer Olympics in Sydney and the 2004 Summer Olympics in Athens. He had the world record at one time in the 200, 400, and 1500.

9. **Aaron Peirsol.** I know it's just one stroke but he is the greatest backstroker in history, male or female. Considering swimming is one of only five sports that have been in every Olympics dating to 1896, that's impressive. He is a three-time Olympian and seven-time Olympic medalist (five gold, two silver).

10. **Alexander Popov**. Perhaps the greatest sprinter in history as he won the 50 AND the 100 free in successive Olympics (1992 and 1996) and held the world record in the 50 for eight years.

1. **Tracy Caulkins**. The most amazing all-around swimmer I have ever seen. She could do it all. In fact, she had the American record in all four strokes at the same time! Three gold medals and, if it were not for the 1980 boycott, it would likely have been a lot more. She's set five world records and sixty three American records.

2. **Janet Evans**. The greatest distance swimmer in history could do it all. Four gold and one silver and world records that stood a generation. She is an amazing swimmer and representative of our sport.

3. **Dawn Fraser**. She held the 100 Free world record for fifteen years and won it in three successive Olympics.

4. **Natalie Coughlin.** Twelve Olympic medals (three gold). Three Olympic Games. First woman to break a minute in the 100 meter back. The list goes on and on.

5. **Yana Klotchkova**. I put her here for her versatility. She won back-to-back 200 and 400 IMs in 2000 and 2004, for a total of four gold medals and one silver in the 800!

6. **Shirley Babashoff**. I would like to put her as number one and she very well would be if it weren't for the East German cheating machine of the 70s. Eight individual Olympic medals and one gold on a relay, six world records and six silver medals that really

should all be gold.

7. **Katie Ledecky.** I know she has only won one Olympic gold medal but after Rio that number will increase and she could be number one. No single swimmer (not named Phelps) has been as dominant in swimming during a four-year period.

8. **Krisztina Egerszegi.** She is a three-time Olympian (1988, 1992 and 1996) and five-time Olympic champion. She is also one of three individuals (Dawn Fraser and Michael Phelps being other two) to have ever won the same swimming event at three consecutive Summer Olympics.

9. **Mary T. Meagher.** Just like Peirsol and Kitajima, she was not only great in butterfly but was the best in history. Her world record in the 100 and 200 fly stood for eighteen and nineteen years, and are considered to be among the greatest sports performances ever.

10. **Jenny Thompson.** She never won an individual gold medal but is one of the most decorated Olympians in history, winning twelve medals, including eight gold medals, in the 1992, 1996, 2000, and 2004 Summer Olympics.